TREE-KANGAROOS
OF AUSTRALIA AND NEW GUINEA

For Charlie Roberts
North Queensland Bushman

TREE-KANGAROOS

OF AUSTRALIA AND NEW GUINEA

Roger Martin

Illustrated by Sue Simpson

CSIRO
PUBLISHING

© Roger Martin 2005

National Library of Australia Cataloguing-in-Publication entry

Martin, Roger William, 1946– .
     Tree-kangaroos of Australia and New Guinea.

     Bibliography.
     Includes index.
     ISBN 0 643 09072 X.

     1. Tree kangaroos – Australia. 2. Tree kangaroos – New Guinea. I. Simpson, Sue. II. CSIRO. III. Title. (Series : Australian natural history series).

     599.22

Available from
CSIRO PUBLISHING
150 Oxford Street (PO Box 1139)
Collingwood VIC 3066
Australia

Telephone: +61 3 9662 7666
Local call: 1300 788 000 (Australia only)
Fax: +61 3 9662 7555
Email: publishing.sales@csiro.au
Web site: www.publish.csiro.au

Front cover
Finsch's Tree-kangaroo *(Dendrolagus inustus finschi)*
Photo by Roger W. Martin
Back cover
Riverine complex forest of the Annan River
Photo by Roger W. Martin
Author photo by Courtney Booker

Set in 10.5/14 Sabon
Cover and text design by James Kelly
Typeset by J&M Typesetting
Printed in Australia by Ligare

Preface

This book is a summary of current knowledge on the biology and natural history of tree-kangaroos. While there are 10 species currently described, readers will find a heavy emphasis placed on the two Australian species, Bennett's Tree-kangaroo (*Dendrolagus bennettianus*) and Lumholtz's Tree-kangaroo (*Dendrolagus lumholtzi*). In a book that purports to be on the tree-kangaroos of both Australia and New Guinea this is an unfortunate bias but it is an accurate reflection of the present state of knowledge. Largely because they are relatively abundant and far more accessible to wildlife biologists, almost all recent field research on tree-kangaroos has been done on Australian species. There is still comparatively little known about the New Guinea species.

Readers will also find that of the two Australian species I focus more on Bennett's Tree-kangaroo, particularly when discussing the finer points of tree-kangaroo natural history. The main reason for this is that it is the species I know best. Apart from a brief period spent working on Scott's and Grizzled Tree-kangaroos in New Guinea, and the odd foray working on Lumholtz's Tree-kangaroo, almost all tree-kangaroo research I have done over the past 15 years has been on this species.

When I started my field studies of Bennett's I wasn't planning a comparative study of all members of the genus. I was simply trying to determine the conservation status of this one species, which was very poorly known at the time. However, as the work progressed and I became more familiar with Bennett's Tree-kangaroo and its habits, 'dendrolagophilia' set in. I realised I was dealing with a truly extraordinary marsupial and this led me to ask broader questions about the biology and origins of the genus as a whole. It is only now, in writing this book and attempting to give plain answers to these questions, that I realise the serendipity involved in selecting Bennett's Tree-kangaroo as a study animal in the first place. It has given me insights into tree-kangaroo biology that I doubt would have been available had I studied any other species.

For a start, Bennett's Tree-kangaroo belongs to the ancestral grade of tree-kangaroos. That is, with its two sister taxa Lumholtz's and the Grizzled Tree-kangaroo, it is thought to be the least differentiated from the original stock of kangaroos that abandoned their terrestrial ways and took to living in the trees. And thus it is directly linked to the big question, the great paradox of kangaroo evolution: why did an animal so beautifully adapted for terrestrial living abandon all to take up an arboreal lifestyle? Knowledge of Bennett's Tree-kangaroo and its natural history has provided some important clues towards an answer to this question.

The most important clues have come from its use of habitat. Bennett's Tree-kangaroo occupies a wide range of habitat types – wider in fact than any other species of tree-kangaroo. Upland montane rainforest was its presumed preferred habitat at the outset of my studies, but Bennett's proved equally populous in the lowland monsoon forests. It even occupied the sparse riverine forests clothing the creeks meandering through the dry country on their way to the Coral Sea.

A major difficulty usually encountered when studying tree-kangaroos is their rareness but, in part because of its widespread habitat, this wasn't the case with Bennett's. As well, populations of Bennett's Tree-kangaroo were both undisturbed and secure in these habitats (most of them being in World Heritage areas). The populations were also free of hunting pressure. Over-hunting is the main reason New Guinea tree-kangaroos are rare and although the indigenous inhabitants of Australia's wet tropics also used to be avid tree-kangaroo hunters, they ceased the practice more than 50 years ago. As a consequence, Bennett's Tree-kangaroo is now populous – probably as populous as it has been since the last Ice Age.

The other great advantage of such a focus on Bennett's Tree-kangaroo, particularly when writing a natural history such as this, is the long period over which it has attracted notice and been written about. It was the first tree-kangaroo reported in Australia and the first to be caught live and held in captivity here. Many eminent zoologists (Richard Semon, George Tate, Hobart Van Deusen) have visited the Bloomfield River district in search of Bennett's Tree-kangaroo and there is an extensive literature of their various quests from which much can be learnt.

For these reasons I hope my bias is understood and appreciated for the insights it provides. Even so, there have been relatively few field studies on tree-kangaroos and we still know very little about them. Few Australians are even aware of their existence. An earlier natural history (by Tim Flannery, Alexandra Szalay and me, with beautiful illustrations by Peter Schouten), published in 1996, reached fewer people than we had hoped, so this current book aims to introduce tree-kangaroos to the wide audience they deserve.

Tree-kangaroos have a notoriously long period of gestation and, in keeping with this, so did this book. Many people have assisted me over the years and I am very much in their debt.

Over the time I spent doing fieldwork in the Bloomfield River area, I received help from many local residents. Pre-eminent among these are Lewis,

Charlie and Edith Roberts from Shipton's Flat and Rob and Ruth Whiston from Gap Creek. My work on Bennett's Tree-kangaroo could not have been done without them. I also thank Viare Kula, Oscar Kirsch, Tom Veitch, Geoff Waldeck and Bruce and Sue Simpson.

I am grateful to John Elliott, Scientific Editor of UNSW Press, for first eliciting and then offering to publish a book on the natural history of tree-kangaroos. Unfortunately the UNSW Press's Natural History series was finished before the book.

The book has been written under a number of different roofs and I am indebted to Peter McCarthy, Arthur Blackham, Amanda Embury and particularly Amy Shima for their hospitality.

I would like to thank William Foley, John Nelson, Will Betz and Lisa Dabek for allowing me access to their unpublished material on tree-kangaroos and for permitting me to quote from it. I am also grateful to Ian Beveridge for giving me some of his precious time to discuss the intricacies of tree-kangaroo parasites. I thank Peter Johnson for allowing me access to his captive animals at Pallarenda, Queensland.

Ian and Keith Stewart were also very generous with their time and expertise in scanning images of tree-kangaroos for me. David Humphrey, from the Department of Photography at Monash University also photographed some material. I would also like to thank Gerald Cubitt, John Nelson and Dan Irby for allowing me to use their photographs.

I am grateful to Tim Flannery for facilitating a couple of trips to New Guinea that allowed me to get a first-hand impression of field research on tree-kangaroos in that country.

I thank the staff of the Australian Museum Library in Sydney for their assistance in providing reference material from some of the rarer books and journals in their collection. I also thank Ralph Schmit, Dermot Henry and Tom Rich from Museum Victoria for locating and making available fossil material in their care.

Michael Kearney, Nicole Kearney and Chris Johnson read and commented on earlier versions of this work and I am particularly grateful to them. As I am to Sue Simpson for the magnificent job she did in drawing the majority of the illustrations in this book.

Finally I would like to thank Amy Shima for her enduring good judgment throughout the many discussions we had about this book, as well as for her support and encouragement during the final stages of its writing.

Roger Martin

Contents

1
A tree-climbing kangaroo?

Some years ago, in a very useful little dictionary of mammal names, Ronald Strahan of the Australian Museum observed that the scientific names of most Australian mammals were derived from either Latin or Greek roots and, assuming one could understand them, these often conveyed useful information about the species. For example, *Dendrolagus*, the name given to the tree-kangaroo genus, is derived from two Greek words – *dendron*, meaning tree, and *lagos*, meaning hare. Strahan mused that while the first part of this name obviously referred to the arboreal lifestyle of the members of the genus, he had no idea why these 'remarkable short-eared, long tailed animals should be compared to hares'.

To understand why, we need to go back to 1826. In that year the Natural History Commission of the Netherlands Indies began sending scientists to the Dutch East Indies to collect natural history specimens, an initiative largely due to Coenraad Temminck, the son of the Treasurer of the Dutch East India Company. He was a wealthy man with an interest in natural history. The East Indies (now Indonesia) comprises thousands of tropical islands and the first group of Dutch scientists to arrive there used a small sailing vessel, *The Triton*, to travel around. When they visited Lobo, on the north-west coastline of New Guinea, they collected four individuals of a mammal that was new to science. According to the local people these animals lived in the trees and were

The drawings of the 'wangoerie' (*Dendrolagus ursinus*) and 'wakera' (*D. inustus*) from Schlegel and Muller's original paper reporting the discovery of these two new species of mammal.

relatively common in the forests of the coastal range. They knew them as 'wangoerie'. The four animals had been raised as pets in local villages and they were taken on board *The Triton* with the intention of shipping them back to Europe alive. Unfortunately, other circumstances intervened and the wangoerie didn't make it.

Even today, Europeans who spend time in the coastal areas of New Guinea usually contract 'fever' (malaria) or experience some sort of debilitating illness. The scientists on board *The Triton* were no exception and many were gravely ill by the time the wangoerie came aboard. Three of the animals were immediately killed to provide fresh meat and broth for the sick men. Dr Salomon Muller was one of the few to survive the voyage and he later reported that the meat of the wangoerie was very tasty, far more so than another macropod species 'fanei' (*Dorcopsis brunii*, Forest Wallaby) eaten earlier in the voyage. He noted how proud the ship's officer was of a special dish that he had prepared for the dying men using this meat, cooking it in the style of 'hazenpeper' (peppered hare).

So, it seems that the *lagus* bit of the scientific name for tree-kangaroo was assigned for gastronomical rather than morphological reasons. The qualities of hare as a game animal have long been appreciated by Europeans and the hungry Dutchmen on board *The Triton* probably recognised a similar 'gaminess' in tree-kangaroo meat when they first caught its smell wafting from the galley. I made the same association when I first encountered its sweet aroma in hunting camps in the Torricelli Mountains of New Guinea.

The scientific name is really most apt and one that indigenous people from both sides of Torres Strait would applaud as they have long recognised tree-kangaroo as one of the finest game animals in the region. The name also serves to remind modern scientists of the main threat to the survival of tree-kangaroos in the wild. Because their flesh is so tasty tree-kangaroos are still hunted relentlessly in most parts of New Guinea. It is never a wise evolutionary strategy to taste good (witness the plight of the dugong) and although the odds may have favoured tree-kangaroos in the past (when there were fewer hunters and larger areas of habitat available), they don't anymore.

History of discovery

In addition to the wangoerie, which was given the scientific name *Dendrolagus ursinus* (referring to the bear-like appearance of what is today known as the Vogelkopt Tree-kangaroo), Salomon Muller and his companions collected a second species of tree-kangaroo in the Lobo district. Known to the locals

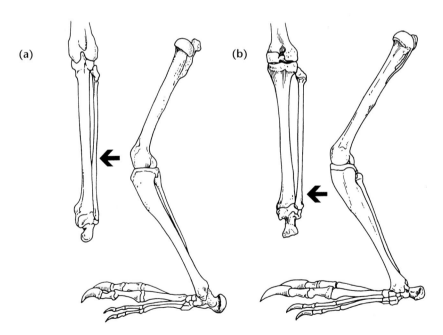

(a)   (b)

The drawings of the hind limbs of the two tree-kangaroo species collected by Salomon Muller and his colleagues in 1826 highlight the different degree of tibio-fibular contact that was to become an important distinguishing characteristic between the two groups of tree-kangaroos. (a) *Dendrolagus inustus*, (b) *D. ursinus*.

as 'wakera', this was the Grizzled Tree-kangaroo (*D. inustus*). Only a single specimen, an old female, was obtained and Muller noted that, apart from its longer tail, the animal was broadly similar in overall appearance to the other species. It wasn't until much later, when describing the skeletal material, that he observed major differences in the long bones (the tibia and fibula) and the ankle bones of the hind limbs of the two species. These, as we will see later, were to prove key characteristics in distinguishing between the two main groups of tree-kangaroos.

Half a century was to pass before another tree-kangaroo species was discovered by Europeans. Surprisingly it wasn't found in New Guinea, but in the rainforests of north Queensland. In 1872 the Queensland Government commissioned William Hann to lead an expedition up Cape York Peninsula to investigate its mineral potential. While passing through rainforest north of the Bloomfield River one of the expedition's Aboriginal guides, Jerry, came upon a very strange wallaby. Hann recorded in his diary that Jerry first saw this animal when it was on the ground '[moving] with the same hopping motion' as a wallaby. However, when disturbed, it climbed a tree and quickly disappeared into the canopy. Jerry had heard of tree-climbing kangaroos before, from his people living further south, around Cardwell. They knew them as 'boongary' and he had often spoken to Hann about them.

William Hann was very sceptical. He wrote in his diary that 'the idea that any kangaroo known to us could climb a tree would be ridiculous'. However, Jerry had accompanied him on many a long journey and 'was faithful and obedient in every difficulty and staunch in every danger' so Hann didn't lightly dismiss what he had to say. They returned the next day to the tree that Jerry had seen the animal climb and found two deep scratches in its bark. Hann observed that the scratches 'were totally different from those of an opossum, which leaves marks as if made with a pin's point' and that they appeared 'to have been made with toes of the hind feet'. Further searching revealed similar scratching on many other trees in the area, leading Hann to believe that the animals were probably plentiful in the area. They didn't see any but did find a complete skeleton which Dr Thomas Tate, another member of the party, enthusiastically collected. But Hann wasn't on a zoological expedition and he didn't see the point of carrying such rubbish around with them. During tough going later on in the trip he insisted that Tate discard it, which he did, and there went the first hard evidence of the presence of tree-kangaroos in Australia.

Jerry wasn't the only one who had heard talk about the unusual tree-climbing kangaroos in the Cardwell area. Rumours had even reached Dr George Bennett at the Australian Museum in Sydney and in 1873 he wrote to the Zoological Society of London suggesting that there may be a tree-kangaroo

Photo: R. Martin

Scratches left in the bark of a gallery forest tree, *Carallia brachiata*, by Bennett's Tree-kangaroo. It was scratches similar to these that lead William Hann to believe that his Aboriginal guide Jerry had indeed seen some type of tree-climbing wallaby in the Bloomfield River district in 1872.

species, similar to those already described from New Guinea, in the rainforests of north Queensland.

In 1880, perhaps influenced by Bennett's speculations, the Reverend Carl Lumholtz came to the Cardwell area to search for tree-kangaroos. Lumholtz was sponsored by the University of Christiania (now Oslo) in Norway and

Lithograph of Lumholtz's Tree-kangaroo (*Dendrolagus lumholtzi*) that accompanied the original description of the species in 1884.

eventually collected four new species of mammals from rainforest in the area. These included a tree-kangaroo that he described as 'the most beautiful mammal' he had seen in Australia. Robert Collet, his colleague from the University, named the species *lumholtzi* in his honour.

As anyone who has tried to capture wild tree-kangaroos will attest, they are exceedingly difficult to find. It took Carl Lumholtz him three months to procure his first specimen and then only after he had enlisted the services of a skilled Aboriginal hunter, Nilgora, and his equally talented dog, Balnglan.

The fourth species of tree-kangaroo, collected in 1883, was found in New Guinea. Its skin came with a shipment of bird skins purchased from a dealer by the Australian Museum. Ornithology was the main passion of the curator, Edward Ramsay. He doesn't appear to have been very interested in mammals, not even beautiful ones. He only gave a perfunctory description and named the species *Dendrolagus dorianus* in honour of the Marquis of Doria 'whose published work on Papuan ornithology he greatly admired'.

Bennett's Tree-kangaroo

The fifth species to be formally described was the tree-kangaroo first seen by Hann's party in 1872. A live specimen was obtained in the vicinity of the Daintree River, which is slightly to the south of the Bloomfield River, in 1886 and sent to the Queensland Museum for identification. Unfortunately the animal didn't travel well. In fact, by the time it reached the Museum, it was long deceased and all that was left was the tattered remains of its skin. With so little material to work with, the museum's curator, the Reverend Charles De Vis, was understandably tentative in his identification. In his published description he only refers to a 'probable new species of *Dendrolagus*'. He didn't have even any material from *D. lumholtzi* in the museum for comparison but, from the description published by Robert Collett in 1884, De Vis thought the bits of skin he had before him were from a different species.

He named it *Dendrolagus bennettianus* in honour of Dr George Bennett who had 'so often insisted on the probability of *Dendrolagus* being endemic to Queensland'. (But perhaps he should have called it after Jerry: Jeanette Covacevich, a former Curator at the Queensland Museum, recently pointed out that it was Jerry, after all, who'd observed the first tree-kangaroo to be formally recorded in Australia.) It wasn't until 1893, when De Vis finally had the opportunity to examine some live tree-kangaroos captured in the Bloomfield River district, that he confirmed *D. bennettianus* as the second tree-kangaroo species living in the rainforests of north Queensland.

W. H. Dudley Le Souef, from the Zoological and Acclimatisation Society of Victoria, had collected these tree-kangaroos. He was a remarkable man and, given the difficulties usually encountered by those trying to collect tree-kanga-roos, he was extraordinarily successful at it. In his first trip to the Bloomfield River he managed to collect six tree-kangaroos in six weeks and to get four of them back to the Melbourne Zoological Gardens alive. On his instruc-tions another 16 were captured later in the following year and also sent to Melbourne Zoo. In 1896 he returned and collected several more, this time from further south around Mount Peter Botte. Captive colonies of tree-kangaroo are rare, even today, and Le Souef's effort must have been somewhat of a coup for Melbourne's Zoological Gardens.

Unfortunately the captive colony did not thrive. In a later account on the history of the zoo, Charles Barrett observed 'our southern climate did not agree with these natives of tropical Queensland'. This is not surprising, given that the animals appear to have been held in an outside enclosure throughout Melbourne's notoriously cold, wet and windy winters. The fact that Le Souef

W. H. Dudley Le Souef, a director of Melbourne's Zoological Gardens, collected several Bennett's Tree-kangaroos for the zoo in the late 19th century.

made several return journeys to north Queensland to collect additional animals suggests that they didn't breed in captivity and that the colony slowly died out. Some recent research provides an interesting digression on the fate of the final few.

The Bennett's Tree-kangaroo exhibit at the Melbourne Zoological Gardens in the early 20th century.

Originally national parks were seen as refuges for all wildlife – not just the locally occurring species. This was the case for Victoria's first national park, at Wilsons Promontory, and in its early years more than a dozen non-endemic species were released there, including a few Bennett's Tree-kangaroos. The two researchers who unearthed this little gem of early conservation practice, Ian Mansergh and the late John Seebeck, didn't ascertain the source of the animals but I suspect they were from the Melbourne Zoo colony. These authors were charitable in their comment that 'the beliefs and endeavours of an earlier generation of conservationists must be viewed in the context of their time' but did go on to observe that the liberation of tropical rainforest mammals onto Wilsons Promontory 'was optimistic, to say the least'. Perhaps they were released with the fond hope that living free would induce them to breed. Or perhaps it was just a misguided act of compassion, letting a few old animals live out the last of their days in the wild.

The carcasses of the two animals that died in transit from Cape York were put to better use. Tree-kangaroos were still rare enough to be of interest to the international scientific community and the bodies of these Bennett's Tree-kangaroos were sent to the Zoological Society in London for further study. One result of this gift was a beautiful lithograph of a young female produced by Smit (Plate 1). Some good science was done as well, with the Prosector of the Zoological Society, Frank Beddard, producing detailed anatomical descriptions of the stomach, intestines, liver, heart and brain of Bennett's Tree-kangaroo.

Returning to Dudley Le Souef, his extraordinary collecting success appears to have been due to the knowledge and expertise of the Aboriginal people from the Bloomfield River area, the Gugu Yalangi. He goes some way towards acknowledging this in his book *Wildlife in Australia*, a compendium of his experiences that appeared a decade after his first expedition to north Queensland. The book contains a photograph of a heavily cicatrised Gugu Yalangi man identified only as Pannican. The caption describes him as 'a native who helped catch the tree wallaby'. The text also refers to what was perhaps the real key to their success – the hunting dog, Merrgo.

Dudley Le Souef had been less forthcoming in an earlier account of his first expedition, which appeared in 1894, the year after he returned to Melbourne with the tree-kangaroos. In it he only acknowledged the help of a local white family, the Hislops. He gave no details of where the animals were found or of how they were captured. At that time the newly appointed curator at the Australian Museum, Edgar Waite, was curious about how so many of these rare animals were caught in such a short time and he corresponded with the Hislop's for details. The younger Hislop, Robert, was a key source in the article that Waite also published on Bennett's Tree-kangaroo in 1894.

If I can digress, that article and the scant information published by Le Souef constituted the entire knowledge of the habits of Bennett's Tree-kangaroo when I first started fieldwork on the species in 1987. I was particularly interested in capture techniques as I planned to fit radio-collars to the tree-kangaroos and as there were no longer any active hunters among the Gugu Yalangi, I would have to catch the animals myself. Robert Hislop said that either he lassoed the animals or quietly climbed up the tree underneath them, seized them by the tail and slipped them into a bag. This use of a lasso didn't sound very different from the way I had caught koalas so, when I headed north on my first field trip, I was confident that I could catch as many tree-kangaroos as I needed for my study.

Alas, it didn't turn out that way. Tree-kangaroos proved to be the most elusive and difficult species to capture that I have ever encountered. After my first futile attempt to noose one I realised that Robert Hislop's account was complete rubbish. I have often pondered his motives for writing it. Perhaps Dud, fearing some competition from the New South Welshmen, had told him not to give anything away. But then again, north Queenslanders have always enjoyed testing the gullibility of southerners, particularly those with scientific pretensions.

A plethora of tree-kangaroos

In 1887, only one year after he had described Australia's second species of tree-kangaroo, Charles De Vis described a third species, *Dendrolagus fulvus*. But his new taxon, as with many of the others to be mentioned in this section, didn't survive the test of time. Differences between tree-kangaroo populations are often considered too slight to warrant species status and *D. fulvus* subsequently proved to be a variant of Lumholtz's Tree-kangaroo. It didn't even become well enough known to warrant a common name. But its description marked the beginning of the phase during which a large number of new species of tree-kangaroos were described

New Guinea was the most fertile ground and Lord Walter Rothschild, an English aristocrat and member of that famous family of financiers, figured prominently in the description of several new species. Lord Rothschild retained his fascination for tree-kangaroos for a very long period. Beginning in 1898 he described *Dendrolagus maximus* and in 1907, together with Forster, Matschie's Tree-kangaroo (*Dendrolagus matschiei*). In the following year Goodfellow's Tree-kangaroo (*Dendrolagus goodfellow*) was described by Oldfield Thomas from the British Museum and Rothschild returned to the fray in 1933 when, with the help of Guy Dollman, he added the new species *Dendrolagus mayri*.

In the late 19th and early 20th centuries the eastern part of New Guinea was a German colony and the Museum für Naturkunde in Berlin acquired a large collection of tree-kangaroo specimens. In his time as Curator of Mammals at the museum, Paul Matschie alone named eight new species and subspecies, including *Dendrolagus buergersi* in 1912 and *Dendrolagus notatus, D. finschi* and *D. keiensis* in 1916.

In 1936 Ellis Troughton and another member of that extraordinary family of natural historians, Gay Le Souef, both from the Australian Museum in Sydney, added two more full species, the Lowland Tree-kangaroo (*Dendrolagus spadix*) and *Dendrolagus deltae*, as well as another subspecies of Doria's Tree-kangaroo, (*Dendrolagus dorianus profugus*), to the 15 species already described from New Guinea. They astutely observed that 'the numerous high mountain ranges and extensive rivers systems' of New Guinea favoured 'the development of many confusingly varied and interrelated forms'. In other words, there were plenty of geographic barriers to isolate populations from each other and over time, this is what leads to the emergence of new forms.

Despite the best efforts of Ellis Troughton and his predecessors, the tree-kangaroo cabinet at the Australian Museum still wasn't full and in the 1990s the incumbent curator, Tim Flannery, made some significant additions. In 1990, with Lester Seri from the Papua New Guinea Department of Environment, he collected and described several new forms from north-western New Guinea. Seri's Tree-kangaroo (*Dendrolagus dorianus stellarum*), from the Star Mountains, was described as a subspecies of Doria's Tree-kangaroo and the 'tenkile' (*Dendrolagus scottae*), which also appeared to be related to Doria's, from the Torricelli Mountains. Another of the new animals, the beautiful Golden-mantled Tree-kangaroo (*Dendrolagus goodfellowi pulcherrimus*) from Mount Sappau at the eastern end of the Torricelli Range, was described as a subspecies of Goodfellow's Tree-kangaroo.

Tree-kangaroo aficionados, such as Jim Menzies from the University of Papua New Guinea, had long wondered about the dearth of described species from seemingly ideal habitat in the central highlands of West Papua. Hence, the 1992 publication of a photograph of a very unusual looking tree-kangaroo from this area aroused considerable interest. It was taken in November 1990 by wildlife photographer Gerald Cubitt. He described the serendipitous way in which yet another species of tree-kangaroo became known to Western science:

My wife Janet and I were travelling on the access road from Tipoeka River to the Freeport copper mine at Tembagapura photographing the wonderful diversity of wild landscape, forest and flora along the steeply ascending route that precedes arrival at his high altitude mining town. At around 8000 ft our 4WD rounded a steep corner and there in front of us walking along the road we came upon a Dani tribesman clad only in his 'holim' (penis sheath) and carrying in his arms two tree kangaroos. One was evidently dead (it appeared to be entirely black) but the other, smaller animal had distinctive black and white markings and was very much alive and alert. It appeared to be a young animal. I prevailed on the tribesman to allow me to take some photographs of him holding it in his arms and then on its own on the verge of the road. The kangaroo was very relaxed and unafraid at my attention and contentedly began to eat some vegetation. The tribesman was apparently hoping to sell the animals to expatriates working at the Freeport mine.

Photo: Gerald Cubitt

This photograph, taken by Gerald Cubitt in November 1990, first alerted the zoological world to the existence of another form of tree-kangaroo in the highlands of West Papua.

It wasn't until he got back to London and showed his photograph to a colleague that Gerald Cubitt realised he had captured the first image of an entirely new species of tree-kangaroo. A few years later Tim Flannery visited the area and, with the help of local hunters, collected several specimens from the nearby Surdiman Range. Known as 'dingiso' by the locals, he formally described the animal, giving it the name *Dendrolagus mbaiso*. As with several of the other recently described species from north coast range of New Guinea, it appears to be related to Doria's Tree-kangaroo.

Even before Tim Flannery's discoveries, tree-kangaroo taxonomy was becoming unwieldy and an overview of the relationships within the group was overdue. The first attempt at a comprehensive taxonomy was made in 1936, by Walter Rothschild and Guy Dollman, but there have been several more recent revisions. Tree-kangaroo taxonomy, however, is a big subject and deserves its own chapter.

2
Tree-kangaroo taxonomy

Taxonomy, the science of classifying organisms, is the oldest of the biological disciplines. Its basic principles were first set down by the Swedish naturalist Carl Gustav Linnaeus in the early 1700s and have remained largely unaltered to the present day. The Linnaen system is hierarchical, with the Species as its fundamental unit. Similar species are grouped together into Genera, similar Genera into Families, Families into Orders, Orders into Classes and Classes into the largest division of the animal kingdom, the Phylum.

The convention is to assign a generic as well as a specific name to each species. All tree-kangaroos, for example, belong to the genus *Dendrolagus*. The Grizzled Tree-kangaroo is *Dendrolagus inustus*, Bennett's Tree-kangaroo *Dendrolagus bennettianus*, and so on for all of the described tree-kangaroo species. Proceeding further up the hierarchy, the tree-kangaroo genus *Dendrolagus* is in the Family Macropodidae (which includes all the large kangaroos). The Macropods, together with all the other marsupials that posses a single pair of functional incisors in the lower jaw, form the Order Diprotodonta. Diprotodonts are members of the Class Mammalia in the Phylum Chordata. When referred to in the formal scientific literature, the name of the describer, the date of publication of the description of the species and the family to which it belongs are often given. Bennett's Tree-kangaroo, for example, appears as *Dendrolagus bennettianus* (Macropodidae) De Vis 1887.

The species concept is fundamental to the Linnean system and, by definition, animals belong to the same species if they are able to interbreed and produce fertile offspring under natural conditions. Unfortunately, reproductive preferences and reproductive outcomes are seldom known for wild populations and this basic information is often unavailable to scientists confronted with variants of an already described species. In classical taxonomy other criteria have to be relied upon and the most important of these are morphological (i.e. to do with the form and structure of the animals).

Taxonomic schemes aim to reflect evolutionary relationships and when morphological characters are used, the underlying assumption is that the more features animals have in common with each other, the more closely related they are.

There are several problems with this approach. One is convergent evolution. Some species, even though they lack a common ancestor, evolve similar characters in response to the similar environmental niches they occupy. Malagasy Aye Ayes and Australian Striped Possums, for example, both feed on insect larvae and both have an elongated digit on their forepaws for hooking these tasty grubs out of their holes. However, this is about the only morphological character they share and they belong to two widely different groups of mammals.

Another problem is the normal spread of morphological variation that occurs in an interbreeding population. With koalas, for example, animals from the colder, southern part of their range are much bigger, have darker coloured fur and are much hairier than their cousins from sunnier climes in the north. But they readily interbreed and therefore they are all regarded as members of a single species, *Phascolarctos cinereus*.

Sorting out relationships becomes even more difficult when dealing with closely related forms. One of the main mechanisms postulated for the evolution of a new species is for a single, large population to be broken up into a series of smaller, discrete populations. Geographical isolation usually leads to reproductive isolation and, over time, both chance and natural selection contribute to small subpopulations diverging from one another. Body sizes may become larger or smaller, colours may change and new behaviours may develop. But how far they diverge depends, among other things, on how intense the pressure to adapt to their new environment is and how long they have been isolated. Populations that have only been separated from each other for a relatively short time may not have diverged much at all.

The challenge for taxonomists is to decide when different populations have diverged far enough to be regarded as different species. How significant, for example, is a change in body size or in the colour of the spots on an animals' tail? Some taxonomists, affectionately known as 'lumpers', choose to ignore any small differences between related populations and lump them together as a single species. Other taxonomists, known as 'splitters', attach greater significance to small differences and assign subspecies status to each subpopulation. The subspecies are then given an additional name to distinguish them from each other and therefore have a trinomial scientific name. The trinomial name of Seri's Tree-kangaroo, for example, is *Dendrolagus dorianus stellarum*. You will notice that there are lots of trinomial tree-kangaroo names.

The hair whorl

In their comprehensive descriptions of *Dendrolagus ursinus*, the first species of tree-kangaroo collected, Schlegel and Muller noted that the lie of the hair on the animals' back, particularly at the top of the shoulders, changed direction and formed a whorl. Years later Edward Ramsay noted a similar hair whorl when he was describing the first specimen of *D. dorianus*.

Table 2.1 Taxonomy of tree-kangaroos proposed by Rothschild and Dollman in 1936

CHARACTERISTIC	GROUP 1	GROUP II	GROUP III
Position of whorl	Centre of back	Root of tail	On shoulders
Coat colour	Red	Light-chocolate–golden brown	Various
	Dendrolagus matschiei (*D. m. matschiei*) (*D. m. xanthotis*) (*D. m. flavidor*)	*Dendrolagus dorianus* (*D. d. dorianus*) (*D. d. notatus*) (*D. d. mayri*)	*Dendrolagus ursinus* (*D. leucogenys*)
			Dendrolagus inustus (*D. i. inustus*) (*D. i. keiensis*) (*D. i. finschi*) (*D. maximus*) (*D. sorongensis*) (*D. schoedei*)
	Dendrolagus goodfellowi (*D. g. goodfellowi*) (*D. g. buergersi*) (*D. g. shawmayeri*)		
			Dendrolagus bennettianus
			Dendrolagus lumholtzi

The species listed in brackets are subspecies recognised by Rothschild and Dollman.
The species listed in small print are no longer recognised as true species.

When Walter Rothschild and Guy Dollman were looking for morphological characteristics with which to distinguish tree-kangaroo species, they seized upon this hair whorl as they were confident it occurred in differed positions (either on the shoulders, in the centre of the back or at the root of tail) in different species. Relying on this single characteristic they reduced the number of species from 15 to seven, which simplified the taxonomy considerably (Table 2.1).

Further taxonomic revisions

In 1948 George Tate from the American Museum of Natural History revised the entire kangaroo family. He divided tree-kangaroos into three groups, but his groupings were very different to those proposed by Rothschild and Dollman. For example, Tate put Bennett's Tree-kangaroo (*D. bennettianus*) in the same group as Doria's (*D. dorianus*) and was strongly of the opinion that the Volgelkopt and Grizzled Tree-kangaroos (*D. ursinus* and *D. inustus*, respectively) were merely different colour phases of the same species. These were serious errors. He couldn't have looked at much of the source material or read Schlegel and Muller's original article which clearly describe the different arrangement of the long bones in the hind limbs of *D. ursinus* and *D. inustus*.

George Tate was a scientist of enormous prestige and this probably influenced many scientists to adopt his tree-kangaroo classification in preference

Table 2.2 Taxonomy of tree-kangaroo proposed by Colin Groves in 1982

Species	Subspecies	Common name
Dendrolagus inustus	D. i. inustus	Grizzled Tree-kangaroo
	D. i. finschi	
Dendrolagus lumholtzi		Lumholtz's Tree-kangaroo
Dendrolagus bennettianus		Bennett's Tree-kangaroo
Dendrolagus ursinus		Black or White-throated Tree-kangaroo*
Dendrolagus matschiei	D. m. matschiei	Matschie's Tree-kangaroo
	D. m. goodfellowi	
	D. m. shawmayeri	
	D. m. buergersi	
	D. m. spadix	
Dendrolagus dorianus	D. d. dorianus	Doria's Tree-kangaroo
	D. d. notatus	
	D. d.mayri	

* *D. ursinus* was given the common name Vogelkopt Tree-Kangaroo in the mid-1990s.

to that of Rothschild and Dollman. However, with the passage of time, it has been justifiably relegated to the dustbin of doubtful science.

In 1982 Colin Groves, from the Department of Prehistory at the Australian National University, published the third major revision of the tree-kangaroo

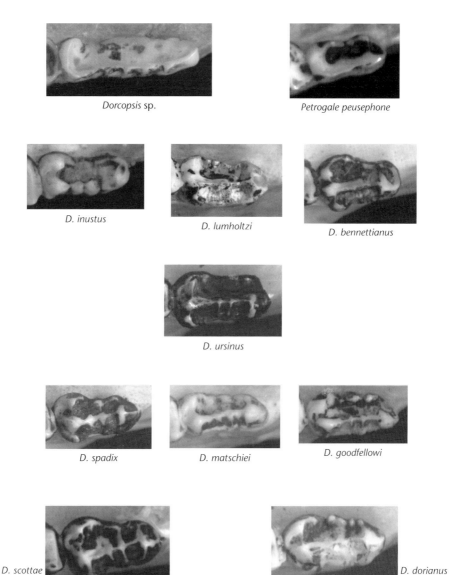

Dorcopsis sp.

Petrogale peusephone

D. inustus

D. lumholtzi

D. bennettianus

D. ursinus

D. spadix

D. matschiei

D. goodfellowi

D. scottae

D. dorianus

Maxillary premolars from the upper jaw (P³) of all the described species of tree-kangaroo together with P³ from two possible ancestral animals, New Guinea forest wallabies (*Dorcopsis* sp.) and the Proserpine Rock Wallaby (*Petrogale persephone*). The premolars are arranged according to the lineage suggested by Groves (1982), from what he considers the ancestral condition, seen in *D. inustus*, *D. lumholtzi* and *D. bennettianus*, in sequence to the *D. dorianus* complex.

genus. Groves had access to much more material than the earlier workers and, in the best traditions of classical taxonomy, used many characteristics to produce his version of tree-kangaroo relationships. He further reduced the original 15 to six species.

In his examination of the teeth, particularly the maxillary premolar of the upper jaw (P^3), Groves found what he considered to be a clear indication of relationships, both among tree-kangaroos and between tree-kangaroos and New Guinea forest wallabies (*Dorcopsis* sp.). The maxillary premolar is a long, narrow blade in both genera and Groves suggested that this tooth, particularly in the Grizzled (*Dendrolagus inustus*) and Lumholtz's (*D. lumholtzi*) Tree-kangaroos, was derived from what he hypothesised was the ancestral condition seen in *Dorcopsis* wallabies. He argued that the premolar of *D. bennettianus* was also derived from the wallaby pattern, even though it had developed somewhat differently to the other two tree-kangaroo species. He further suggested that progressive elaborations from this ancestral condition were evident in a sequence running from the Vogelkopt Tree-kangaroo (*D. ursinus*) through Goodfellow's (*D. goodfellowi*) to Matschie's Tree-kangaroo (*D. matschiei*). Doria's Tree-kangaroo (*D. dorianus*) was seen as a development branching off from the *D. goodfellowi* pattern

Big feet

The Dutch zoologist A. M. Husson, from the Museum of Natural History in Leiden, was the first to observe differences in the feet of the various tree-kangaroo species. He noted that the middle toe of the Grizzled Tree-kangaroos (*D. inustus*) was much longer than the lateral toe, whereas these toes were more equal in length in the Vogelkopt Tree-kangaroos (*D. ursinus*). Colin Groves thought that the arrangement in *D. inustus* resembled the typical macropod pattern and when he checked the other tree-kangaroo species, he found he could split them into two groups based on this characteristic. He put *D. inustus* together with the two Australian species (*D. lumholtzi* and *D. bennettianus*) into one – the long-toed group – and the rest of the New Guinea species, which had toes of more equal length, into the other.

When he compared foot lengths (standardised against head–body length) for each species, Groves found that the tree-kangaroo species fell into the same two groups for this characteristic as well. The Grizzled Tree-kangaroo (*D. inustus*) and the two Australian species, Lumholtz's and Bennett's Tree-kangaroos, were relatively long-footed while the rest were short-footed.

Groves also found that tail lengths differed between species but this character didn't divide the species into the same groups as for their foot lengths. The two Australian species had the longest tails (relative to their body length),

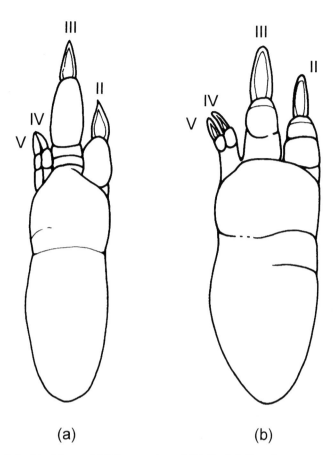

Drawings of the hind feet of (a) Bennett's and (b) Doria's Tree-kangaroos showing the difference in the relative length of the middle toe. This is one of the characteristics used to separate tree-kangaroos into two groups.

but Grizzled Tree-kangaroos had a shorter tail than both the Goodfellow's and Matschie's Tree-kangaroos.

Groves also revisited the hair whorl and was less enthusiastic than Rothschild and Dollman on its value as a taxonomic character. He found its position to be variable in some species and very poorly expressed in others.

Yet another taxonomic revision

In the 1990s, while he was curator of the mammal collection at the Australian Museum in Sydney, Tim Flannery collected extensively in New Guinea and discovered two new species and two additional subspecies of tree-kangaroos.

In describing one of the new animals, a subspecies of Goodfellow's (*D. goodfellowi pulcherrimus*), Flannery reviewed relationships within the entire group and produced a taxonomy that differed from that of Colin Groves.

Table 2.3 Taxonomy of tree-kangaroos proposed by Tim Flannery in 1996

Species	Subspecies	Common name
Dendrolagus bennettianus		Bennett's Tree-kangaroo
Dendrolagus lumholtzi		Lumholtz's Tree-kangaroo
Dendrolagus inustus	D. i. inustus	Grizzled Tree-kangaroo
	D. i. finschi	Finsch's Tree-kangaroo
Dendrolagus ursinus		Vogelkopt Tree-kangaroo
Dendrolagus goodfellowi	D. g. goodfellowi	Goodfellow's Tree-kangaroo
	D. g. buergersi	Timboyok
	D. g. pulcherrimus	Golden-mantled Tree-kangaroo
Dendrolagus matschiei		Matschie's Tree-kangaroo
Dendrolagus spadix		Lowland Tree-kangaroo
Dendrolagus dorianus	D. d. dorianus	Doria's Tree-kangaroo
	D. d. mayri	Wondiwoi Tree-kangaroo
	D. d. notatus	Ifola
	D. d. stellarum	Seri's Tree-kangaroo
Dendrolagus scottae		Tenkile
Dendrolagus mbaiso		Dingiso

Groves had previously lumped all of the Goodfellow's subspecies together with the Lowland Tree-kangaroo (D. *spadix*) into one group and regarded them all as subspecies of Matchie's Tree-kangaroo. Tim Flannery reversed this and restored D. *goodfellowi* and D. *spadix* to full species status. He also revived a number of the subspecies originally erected by Rothschild and Dollman in their 1936 taxonomy. In doing so he acknowledges that these so-called 'ornate' tree-kangaroos present a challenge to taxonomists. Paramount among the difficulties is the limited number of specimens available. The enormous variability of colour patterns between individuals is also a problem as fur colour is notoriously unreliable as a taxonomic character. These complexities aside, Tim Flannery's taxonomy constitutes a more informed view that any of the previous attempts.

One or two lineages?

Tim Flannery also raises the question whether tree-kangaroos comprise more than one lineage. Herman Schlegel and Salomon Muller were the first to note the significant difference between D. *ursinus* and D. *inustus* in the anatomy of their hind limbs. In neither animal did the tibia enclose the long, narrow bone of the hind limb (the fibula), as it does in terrestrial kangaroos, but was separate from it. They observed that this condition was far more pronounced in *D. ursinus* than in *D. inustus* (see drawings on page 3).

Tim Flannery attributes a functional significance to this anatomical characteristic, arguing that the reduction in contact between the two long bones allows for greater rotation of the hind foot, which enhances gripping and climbing ability. He suggests this is a major difference between tree-kangaroos species and uses it as a key characteristic for dividing them into two groups, one 'primitive' and the other more highly adapted.

He lumps together the two Australian species, *D. lumholtzi* and *D. bennettianus*, with one of the New Guinea species, *D. inustus*, as the 'primitive' group and considers the remainder of the New Guinean species to be a more highly adapted group. He goes so far as to suggest that these two groups of tree-kangaroos may even represent separate lineages, with all of the New Guinea species descended from an ancestor of the 'primitive' Grizzled Tree-kangaroo.

Is this a possibility? Well, maybe, but let's look at another source of evidence.

Recent insights from genetics

It was only a matter of time before the geneticists had a go at resolving the tantalising problem of tree-kangaroo taxonomy. Jocelyn Bower and Mark Eldridge, from the Department of Biological Sciences at Macquarie University, recently did so. They based their phylogenetic study on a very small section of the tree-kangaroo genome – a fragment of DNA from a mitochondrial gene. (Mitochondria are cell organelles that have their own genetic material. They are passed down the generations via the maternal line only and their genetic material is therefore highly conserved.)

The bulk of the material that Bower and Eldridge analysed was from the two Australian species, *D. lumholtzi* and *D. bennettianus*. They had limited material from six New Guinea species, namely *D. dorianus* (two subspecies), *D. inustus*, *D. goodfellowi*, *D. matschiei*, *D. mbasio* and *D. spadix*.

Their analysis strongly supported a close relationship ('sister taxons') between the two Australian species, which was consistent with Tim Flannery's taxonomy. However, the differences between the mitochondrial DNA of Bennett's and Lumholtz's Tree-kangaroos were great enough to suggest that the two species had diverged from a common ancestor a very long time ago, certainly long before the last glacial maxima of 18 000 years ago. This climatic event is thought to have caused a severe contraction of Australia's rainforests, fragmented the distribution of much of the fauna occupying it and possibly initiated the geographic isolation that eventually leads to the emergence of new species.

Bower and Eldridge also suggested that the mitochondrial DNA of the New Guinea species *D. inustus* was basal to that of *D. lumholtzi* and *D. bennettianus*, implying that it had evolved before either of the Australian species. Their data supporting this were fairly weak and such a phylogeny would be the reverse of what Tim Flannery proposed (he had the Australian tree-kangaroos as the ancestral group) but it is still a very interesting result. It implies one rather than two lineages of tree-kangaroos, but I will return to it later, in the discussion of tree-kangaroo evolution, in Chapter 5.

Bower and Eldridge were less conclusive in sorting out the relationships among the rest of the New Guinea species, largely because of the small amount of material they had to work with. Their analysis supported Tim Flannery's view of *D. goodfellowi*, *D. matschiei* and *D. spadix* as closely related species but they couldn't resolve the relationship between the other New Guinea species he'd recently discovered, *D. mbasio*, and the complex of similar-looking animals all described as subspecies of Doria's Tree-kangaroo. They were perplexed by the large genetic distance they found between two of these subspecies, *D. dorianus stellarum* and *D. d. notatus*.

Future taxonomic revisions

Future systematists will no doubt take up the challenges presented by tree-kangaroo taxonomy. Genetic investigations have barely begun and once the tree-kangaroo DNA becomes available, there will be further revisions. These will undoubtedly clarify some relationships but, if the history of genetic studies of their close relatives the rock-wallabies is any guide, the exact nature of the relationships between some species of tree-kangaroo will be problematic. A precise taxonomy of tree-kangaroos, like the tree-kangaroos themselves, will probably remain elusive.

3

Adaptations for an arboreal life

For more than 20 years the late Stephen Jay Gould, the eminent American palaeontologist, wrote monthly essays for *Natural History Magazine*. Most were in the general area of evolutionary theory and his favourite theme was the quirky and paradoxical nature of natural selection. According to Gould, most of the forms encountered in nature are not optimal designs but structures that have been 'cobbled together' from available components to adequately perform the needed function. Form, in other words, is dictated as much by ancestry as it is by function.

And so it is with tree-kangaroos. On first encountering these amazing beasts Alfred Russel Wallace immediately recognised their affinity with terrestrial kangaroos:

> *They differ chiefly from the ground-kangaroo in having a more hairy tail, not thickened at the base, and not used as a prop; and by the powerful claws on the fore-feet, by which they grasp the bark and branches, and seize the leaves on which they feed. They move along by short jumps on their hind-feet, which do not seem particularly well adapted for climbing trees.*

Today, zoologists believe that the basic body shape of tree-kangaroos was inherited from a terrestrial ancestor that emerged sometime during the harshly arid times of the early Pliocene. The primary ecological force that shaped these terrestrial kangaroos was their need to travel rapidly and efficiently across wide tracts of dry, sparsely vegetated country. Their mode of locomotion, called bipedal hopping or, more technically, 'ricochetal saltatory locomotion' as it essentially involves the animal propelling itself along on the toes of the hind feet, is seen as the key to their evolutionary success. It sounds like a bizarre way to travel and, as anyone witnessing it for the first time will testify, it is. But it is exceptionally energy efficient. In most quadruped mammals, energy expenditure increases with running speed, but not so with kangaroos. Once they get up on their toes and start hopping, they are able to harness the energy stored in the large, elastic tendons of the hind limbs. As their weight comes down on the toe the tendon is stretched and energy is stored and then used as the animal bounds forward. By this means a kangaroo can comfortably traverse a large distance for a relatively small expenditure of energy.

Over millions of years, natural selection favoured anatomical adaptations that improved the efficiency of this bipedal hopping. Large hind limbs, long hind feet (*macro pods*) with prominent fifth toes and long, muscular tails (to counterbalance the thrust generated by the hind limbs) resulted. This was the basic anatomy inherited by the ancestral tree-kangaroos. However, when they abandoned their terrestrial paths for a life in the trees, natural selection was faced with the task of constructing an efficient tree climber from what was, in effect, a two-legged greyhound. In this chapter I will describe how the basic kangaroo form was adapted to achieve this.

Forelimbs and forepaws

Terrestrial kangaroos use their forelimbs for a range of manipulatory purposes, with feeding, fighting and fornicating prominent among them. The overriding evolutionary trend, however, was to reduce front-end mass and trim the body for more efficient bipedal locomotion. Hence, most of the smaller kangaroos are relatively light in the forequarters, with a reduction in the size of the forelimbs as one consequence of this streamlining. The resulting, almost atrophied, appearance of the forearms is a striking feature of many wallabies.

This would not be a very useful condition for tree-kangaroos because they depend heavily on their forearms to pull themselves up into the trees and so they need to be large and well-muscled. As a consequence, the pronounced size difference between the fore- and hind limbs seen in most wallabies is not evident in tree-kangaroos.

A more radical adaptation, however, is seen in the size and shape of the claws on the forepaws of tree-kangaroos. Most macropods have strongly clawed forepaws but claw development in tree-kangaroos is extreme. They

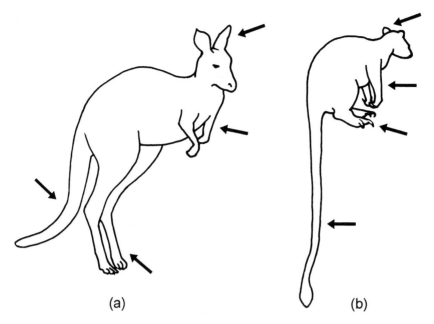

Outlines of (a) the terrestrial kangaroo and (b) the tree-kangaroo reproduced at approximately the same size. The arrows indicate the main anatomical points at which tree-kangaroos diverge from their terrestrial cousins – the ear, forelimb, hind foot and tail.

are not only much longer than those of terrestrial kangaroos but are also wickedly curved. Their main function is to enhance the grip of the tree-kangaroo when it is climbing, particularly when gripping onto vines and smaller branches. But, surprisingly, they also come into play when tree-kangaroos are manipulating items of food.

One would think that long claws would inhibit manual dexterity, but Andrew Iwaniuk, from Monash University, has shown that this certainly isn't the case for tree-kangaroos. He examined how two species of tree-kangaroo, *Dendrolagus lumholtzi* and *D. matschiei*, handled their

The forepaw of a Bennett's Tree-kangaroo showing the curved claws and the shape of the pads.

food and found that, despite their long claws, both species had surprisingly good manual dexterity, with *D. matschiei* even showing some independent movement of the digits.

An unexpected result from Iwanuik's study was that both tree-kangaroo species, when reaching for food, showed considerable freedom of movement of the shoulder and arm. This was far greater than what has been reported for any other macropod species and he thought it resulted from a suite of adaptations to the muscles of the shoulder girdle. Feeding aside, this freedom of movement would also be very useful to the animals when undertaking vertical climbs.

The other main adaptive change to the forepaws is in the size and structure of the pads. They are large, extending down onto the wrist in some species, and covered with small tuberculations (papillae, akin to those on the rubber face of a table tennis bat) that are thought to aid grip when climbing.

Hind limbs and hind paws

Tree-kangaroos use a range of methods to get around, including bipedal hopping. They have retained the enlarged hind limbs of their terrestrial ancestors, but their development, particularly of the flexor and extensor muscles,

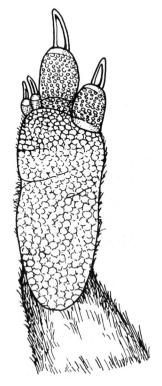

is not as pronounced and they are not capable of anywhere near the hopping speeds achieved by terrestrial kangaroos.

Their hind feet show the typical macropod pattern. The foot is dominated by the enlarged 4th and, to a lesser extent, the 5th digit; while the 1st digit (the hallux) is absent and the 2nd and 3rd digits are reduced in size and bound together in a syndactylous condition. (Syndactyly is when two digits are fused together and appear as a single toe with two toe nails.) The feet differ markedly from those of terrestrial kangaroos by being short, extremely broad and surmounted with a long curved claw on each digit.

The pad of the hindfoot isn't divided into parts, as in terrestrial kangaroos, but forms a single, large and somewhat protuberant whole covered with the same prominent tuberculations seen on the pads

The hind paw of a Bennett's Tree-kangaroo showing the claws and protuberant tuberculated pads.

of the forefeet. Again, the fleshy nature of the pad, together with the tuberculations, presumably enhance the tree-kangaroos' grip when climbing and walking about on branches in the canopy.

There are other adaptations to the hind limbs, particularly to the ankle bones, but these are less obvious. The main ankle bones, the astragalus and calcaneum, are morphologically very complex structures and, unless one is conversant with osteology, descriptions of the normal macropod pattern and the variations seen in tree-kangaroos are difficult to comprehend. Nicholas Bishop, from Flinders University in South Australia, has produced a masterful study of the subject. He found the ankle bones of Bennett's Tree-kangaroo extremely broad when compared to a 'typical' macropod (e.g. Red Kangaroo, *Macropus rufus*) and considers them more reminiscent of a possum or koala than a macropod. Overall, he concludes that the complex of bones in the ankle joint of Bennett's allows greater freedom of movement of the ankle compared with other kangaroos, which is consistent with their arboreal habits.

Tails

Possums, those most inherently arboreal of marsupials, have prehensile tails. That is, they can use their tail tip to grip things and do so most dexterously, as if they had an extra paw. But the tails of tree-kangaroos are not prehensile and they mainly use them as a balancing aid when moving around in the canopy.

When I have seen Bennett's Tree-kangaroos doing this they remind me of a high wire walker with a balancing pole. When traversing thin branches or climbing along vines, they stiffen their tail and hold it rigidly beneath them, presumably to counterbalance the weight of their upper body. Sometimes this isn't the most graceful of manoeuvres, especially when they are trying to hurry along. Then they often end up lurching around with their tail gyrating wildly beneath them, fighting to maintain balance and avoid crashing to the ground.

As Colin Groves observed, tail lengths differ markedly between tree-kangaroo species. In the ancestral species (Bennett's, Lumholtz's and the Grizzled), as well as in Goodfellow's Tree-kangaroo, tails are remarkably long – up to 15% longer than the combined length of their head–body (HB length). Of the other species, both Matschie's and Vogelkopt Tree-kangaroos have shorter tails, about the same as their HB lengths, whereas animals in the Doria's group have tails about 20% shorter than their HB length. Precisely how these species use their tails hasn't been described but tail length probably reflects how much time each species spends in the canopy. The short-tailed *dorianus* group, for example, appear to be the most terrestrial of the tree-kangaroos.

A final point about tails is how tree-kangaroos use them when they are hopping. The muscular tail of a large terrestrial kangaroo plays an important role in the mechanics of hopping because it counters the great rotational thrust generated by the hind limbs, particularly when the animal is moving along at speed. Tree-kangaroos, when they hop bipedally, usually do so at a gentle pace: more like 30 kph than the 60-plus kph of large terrestrial kangaroos. There isn't a lot of rotational thrust to counteract so tree-kangaroos tend to carry their tail in the rock-wallaby style, arched up and forward, like a large question mark. But if they are on the ground and fleeing in a blind panic, it trails straight out behind them, a habit that probably accounts for the occasional sightings of 'tigers' in the rainforests of north Queensland. The tails of tree-kangaroos are of big cat proportions and when you catch a fleeting glance of one bounding along the forest floor with its tasselled tail streaming out behind it, it could easily be mistaken for a big cat.

Tail colouration

One other aspect of tree-kangaroo tails in which natural selection appears to have taken a hand is in their colouration; or more precisely, in how the colour is distributed on the upper and lower surfaces of the tail.

Tail colouration varies between tree-kangaroo species. The tails of Vogelkopt Tree-kangaroos are the same colour as the body and those of the Goodfellow's are patterned similarly to the body. In most of the other species the tails are a lighter colour than the body. The two Australian species are notable exceptions to this. Juvenile Lumholtz's and Bennett's Tree-kangaroos have entirely black tails, but the adult's tails are bicoloured. The lower surface retains the black juvenile colour whereas the upper surface slowly lightens until it's the colour of the adult body fur. This is the reverse of what is usually seen in other mammals with bicoloured tails where it's usually the upper surface that's darkest (Plate 6(b)).

Edgar Waite, from the Australian Museum, first noticed this in Bennett's Tree-kangaroo. He thought that it was related to the animal's resting posture because, when Bennett's rests up in the canopy, it sits with its tail forward, passing it under its body and between its legs. In this position the paler surface of the tail faces downwards. From personal experience I can say that this adds to the difficulties of spotting tree-kangaroos in the canopy. Could it be a form of camouflage against a diurnal predator looking up from the ground? I've often speculated on this and what this predator might be. But more on that later.

Ears

The short, bear-like ears of tree-kangaroos differ strikingly from those of their terrestrial cousins. However, in this case, it may be that the terrestrial and not the arboreal kangaroos have diverged from the ancestral condition. Ears aren't preserved in the fossil record, so we don't really know what those of ancestral kangaroos looked like. But we do know how terrestrial kangaroos use them today.

Terrestrial kangaroos, particularly the large grazing animals that live in open habitat, don't have any safe haven in which to hide from predators. Instead they must rely on alertness and fleetness of foot. When you look at a group of large kangaroos grazing, one of them is always upright and looking around. When this individual puts its head down to graze, another usually puts it head up. What they are doing is looking, listening and smelling for any sign of a potential predator, such as a dingo or human hunter. Hearing is perhaps their most acute sense and if you look closely you'll see that when they are upright their ears rotate like radar dishes. Terrestrial kangaroos probably evolved enlarged ears because of the importance of acute hearing in detecting predators. Tree-kangaroos, although they seem to have reasonable hearing, are probably less reliant on it than terrestrial kangaroos and there has been little evolutionary need for them to have large ears. Large ears could also be a great nuisance when pushing through thick clumps of foliage in the forest canopy.

Modes of locomotion

Dr Udo Ganslosser, from the University of Erlangen-Nurnberg, has made careful observations of the modes of locomotion used by tree-kangaroos, particularly Doria's (*D. dorianus*) and Grizzled (*D. inustus*) Tree-kangaroos held in German zoos.

He observed that Doria's Tree-kangaroos tended to rely on bipedal walking (even walking backwards when needed) when on the ground and only resorted to bipedal hopping to move faster. In contrast, Grizzled Tree-kangaroos seldom walked when on the ground but hopped bipedally most of the time, even when they only wanted to cover a short distance.

Both species converted to quadrupedal mode when above ground and walking/climbing along thin branches. Grizzled Tree-kangaroos tended to be more reliant on bipedal hopping when moving on the larger boughs whereas Doria's only hopped when they were in a hurry.

From this work one could conclude that Doria's, and by implication the entire 'derived group' of tree-kangaroos, are more adept at both bipedal and quadrupedal walking than the more ancestral species, represented by Grizzled Tree-kangaroos in Ganslosser's study. From my own observations of captive Lumholtz's Tree-kangaroo's, (also members of the ancestral group) I suspect that any difference in these capabilities may only be slight. Lumholtz's appears capable of the full range of movements, including walking backwards in the bipedal mode. The differences in locomotory preferences observed by Udo Ganslosser may simply reflect Doria's more terrestrial habits.

Climbing ability

Dr Ganslosser also made precise measurements of the climbing ability of tree-kangaroos. Once again he used zoo animals and he compared their vertical

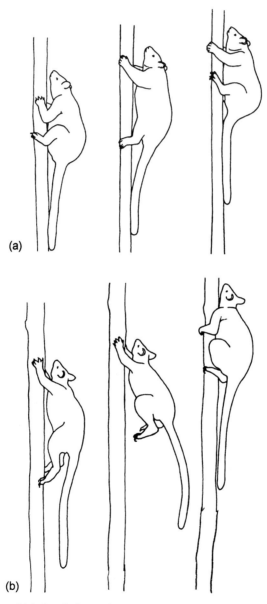

(a)

(b)

Sequence of moves of (a) *Dendrolagus dorianus* and (b) *D. goodfellowi* when climbing a vertical pole (redrawn from Ganslosser 1980, 1981).

tree-climbing ability up a 'standard' artificial tree. He did this for four species: *D. inustus*, *D. goodfellowi*, *D. matschiei* and *D. dorianus*.

First he filmed the animals climbing and from the film he measured such things as body shortening, the distance of the animal's centre of gravity from the tree, the horizontal and vertical distances between the points of contact of the fore- and hind feet, as well as the amplitude, flexion and extension of the joints of the fore- and hind limbs. He interpreted his results in the light of the different body proportions of the species, as well as of their behavioural repertoires.

Ganslosser's main conclusions were that *D. matschiei* was the best vertical climber followed by *D. goodfellowi* and *D. inustus; D. dorianus* was the least adept and although this may be, in part, because it was the largest and heaviest species. Udo Ganslosser concluded that Doria's was better adapted for living on the ground.

In a later investigation of the skeletal anatomy of the same four species, particularly of the robustness of their limb bones and muscle insertions, he found that the two species that seemed to be best adapted for vertical climbing (i.e. Matschie's and Goodfellow's Tree-kangaroos) both showed adaptations that favoured 'strength' rather than 'stride'. From his examination of their skeletons, Ganslosser also reported that the fore- and hind feet of tree-kangaroos seemed to have a greater range of mobility than those of terrestrial macropods.

Although Dr Ganslosser didn't have the opportunity to assess the climbing ability of the other two ancestral species, Lumholtz's and Bennett's Tree-kangaroos, I suspect that they would have also ranked with the Grizzled among the less well-adapted. However, it should be borne in mind that this really is a matter of degree and shouldn't be interpreted as meaning that the ancestral group of tree-kangaroos are by any means inept at climbing trees. Having often seen wild Bennett's Tree-kangaroos swaying around in the upper branches of emergent rainforest trees, some 45 metres above the forest floor, I am very impressed with both their climbing ability and their nerve. With the possible exception of animals from the Doria's group, all of the tree-kangaroos are relatively adept at climbing, even if Matschie's and Goodfellow's are the current pole-climbing champions.

4
The rainforest canopy: A bountiful world

Rainforests are among the most diverse ecosystems on Earth. The equatorial rainforests of Borneo, Central Africa and South America are the richest but the rainforests of New Guinea, where most tree-kangaroo species occur, are not far behind. All of them are certainly more diverse than the drier rainforests of northern Australia – but even those forests are far from impoverished. The rainforests in north Queensland, for example, where Australia's two species of tree-kangaroo live, contain 1380 species of trees and shrubs representing 605 plant genera. This total jumps to 1824 species (representing 855 genera) when vines and epiphytes are included. Compared with the forests of southern Australia or indeed with the temperate forests of the entire continents of Europe and North America, this is huge diversity.

Many of the trees and shrubs and most of the vine and epiphyte species in these north Queensland rainforest are not endemic to Australia but have a broad Malesian distribution (i.e. they also occur in New Guinea, Indonesia, the Philippines, the Malay Peninsula, Thailand and Vietnam). Where they originated, be it the southern super-continent of Gondwana or the northern super-continent of Laurasia, is still a topic of dispute among botanists (there seem to be as many opinions as there are shades of green in the canopy). But origins aside, the huge quantities of leaves, flowers and fruits they produce are an abundant resource for herbivores such as tree-kangaroos.

Tropical rainforests are not uniform in composition or diversity. There are 13 types recognised in north Queensland and the composition of the forest at Shipton's Flat, where I studied Bennett's Tree-kangaroo, gives an impression of diversity in just one type. This forest, classified as a complex notophyll vine forest, contains some 250 species of trees and shrubs and another 20 or so species of epiphytes (mainly ferns and orchids) as well an intricate tangle of some 63 species of vines up in the canopy. The 'notophyll' refers to the predominantly small size of the leaves on all of these plants. It is also a monsoon forest and many of these species are deciduous, shedding a considerable proportion of their leaves in the dry season.

The botanical richness of their habitat raises a number of interesting questions about how tree-kangaroos use it. Pre-eminent among these is, what, specifically, do they eat? They obviously have a great variety of potential foods to choose from. Are they fruit or foliage eaters? If the latter, are they generalist folivores that partake widely from this green cornucopia or are they fussy specialists (similar to koalas)? And if they are koala-like, which particular plant species are important to them? The answers to these questions lead on to other questions about the value of different types of forest to tree-kangaroos. Do they all support comparable numbers or are tree-kangaroos more abundant in some forest types? Questions such as these are especially significant when it comes to making decisions about conserving high-value tree-kangaroo habitat, as we will see in Chapter 10.

But let me begin this discussion about the diet of tree-kangaroos with a description of their digestive equipment – that is, their teeth and gut.

Digestive system of tree-kangaroos

Teeth

The teeth of tree-kangaroos follow the basic macropod pattern; that is, on the upper jaw there are three incisors, a single, vestigial canine, a single premolar and four molars. The lower jaw lacks the canine and only has a single, blade-like incisor but otherwise has the same arrangement of premolars and molars. As is the case with other kangaroos, the first premolars that erupt on the upper jaw – designated P^1 and P^2 – are deciduous and shed at an early age. They are replaced by a single, permanent premolar (P^3).

Tree-kangaroo premolars have many cusps and cutting edges and are more complex than those seen in terrestrial kangaroos. They also differ between species, which makes them useful for taxonomic studies (see figure on p. 19). The

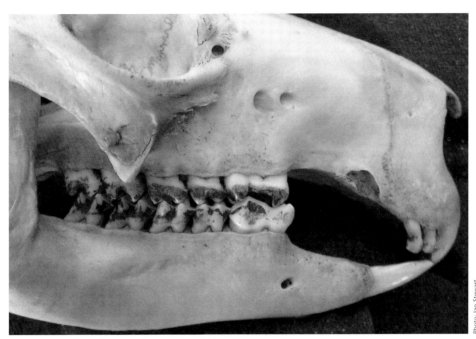

Photo: Ian Stewart

The occluded teeth row of a Bennett's Tree-kangaroo

premolars of the Grizzled Tree-kangaroo (*Dendrolagus inustus*) are by far the simplest and not very different to the pattern seen in one of the presumed tree-kangaroo ancestors, the Rock Wallaby.

The primary role of the incisors and premolars is to gather and manipulate food. The incisors are used to grip and even pluck leaves from the branch. Alternatively, the stem of the leaf is severed by the cutting blade of the premolar. Once the leaf is in the mouth the molars grind it into a fine paste, which is swallowed for further digestion in the gastrointestinal tract.

The molars of all tree-kangaroo species are rather low crowned in comparison with other kangaroos. The large terrestrial kangaroos have extremely high-crowned molars, thought to be an adaptation for feeding on grasses, which have a high content of silica and are very abrasive. Leaf is much softer fare.

Gastrointestinal tract

The structure of the tree-kangaroo gut differs little from the basic kangaroo pattern. Kangaroos are similar in their digestive physiology to ruminants (e.g. cows) – that is, they retain food in their stomach for a long time and rely on an extensive microbial fauna to help digest it. They need a large stomach for this. Kangaroo stomachs are divided into several compartments with each compartment having a different function. The first compartment, the forestomach, is

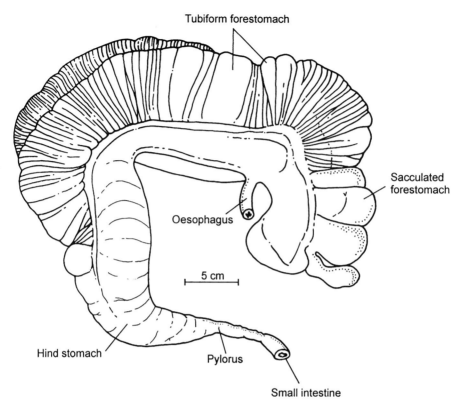

A typical macropod stomach.

sacculated and this permits a concertina-like expansion to accommodate the food ingested during a night's feeding. The next section of the stomach is tube-like (tubiform forestomach) and most of the microbial fermentation takes place here. The hind stomach is lined with a gland-rich mucosa and the process of absorbing the products of digestion begins here.

The tree-kangaroo gut was first described by the English anatomist Sir Richard Owen in 1852 but, probably because it appeared to differ little from the gut of other kangaroos, it aroused little zoological interest. Only in recent years has Tim Flannery had a closer look and found differences between species. The gut of Lumholtz's Tree-kangaroo appears to be the least modified and comparable in its overall structure to the gut of the Grazing Wallaroo (*Macropus robustus*). In Doria's Tree-kangaroo the tubiform forestomach is relatively shorter and the gland-rich hind stomach larger.

Flannery also observed considerable differences between species in other regions of the digestive tract. Finsch's Tree-kangaroo (*D. inustus finschi*), for example, has a remarkably long small intestine and Doria's Tree-kangaroos has a relatively long caecum.

Diet of New Guinea tree-kangaroos

Captive animals

There has been very little fieldwork done on tree-kangaroos in New Guinea and until fairly recently our knowledge of their diet was largely restricted to incidental observations by early naturalists and collectors. In a paper published in 1958 Husson and Rappard summarised what was then known about the feeding habits of the Vogelkopt Tree-kangaroo (*D. ursinus*). Most of their observations were of semi-captive animals, living outside their natural range and with access to exotic garden plants, so they are not much help in understanding the feeding habits of wild tree-kangaroos. However, they do convey the overriding impression that this species of tree-kangaroo, at least, has a very broad diet.

One of these tree-kangaroos fed almost exclusively on the ripe fruit and leaves of a particular fig tree. Another, allowed to roam freely in the garden and adjoining forest of a house at Manokwari (the old Dutch administrative capital on the north coast of West Papua), favoured the leaves, twigs and bark from an introduced White Mulberry (*Morus alba*) – the very same mulberry species whose leaf was once the staple food of silkworms in the Chinese silk industry. This particular tree-kangaroo also fed on the leaves of a species of *Artocarpus* – a relative of the breadfruit tree. A third animal liked to eat flowers, especially those from a Scarlet Wisteria (*Sesbania grandiflora*) growing in the garden.

Another source of dietary information for New Guinea tree-kangaroos is from hand-raised animals. When adult tree-kangaroos are killed by hunters, their pouch young are often kept alive to be hand-raised back in the villages. Here they learn to eat whatever food is given to them. In the Torricelli Mountains, semi-captive Finsch's Tree-kangaroos (*D. inustus finschi*) are largely fed on vegetables, but the foliage of the 'tu-lip' (two-leaf) or Spanish Joint Fir (*Gnetum gnemon*), a common tree around the villages, is an important natural food for them. The young leaves are highly nutritious (>7% protein), so much so that it is widely used as a green vegetable by the villagers themselves.

Knowledge of the hunters

Hunters are usually knowledgeable about the habits of their prey and I found that Olo men, who are the traditional owners of parts of the Torricelli Mountains and hunt both Scott's and Grizzled Tree-kangaroos, knew many of the food plants used by these species. They were happy to point out these plants when I walked through the forest with them. They had local names for all of the plants but unfortunately many were unknown to science and often I wasn't able to assign a botanical name. One tree that animals ate both the leaves and fruit from was undoubtedly a species of fig (*Ficus*). Of greater interest to me, however, was the evidence of tree-kangaroo's feeding on the ground. In a boggy area there was fresh tree-kangaroo dung scattered around a patch of nettles and a couple of species, probably *Elatostema* and *Procris* (Urticaceae), were obviously being browsed by the tree-kangaroos.

Tim Flannery has both interviewed hunters and followed a captive juvenile Scott's Tree-kangaroo (*D. scottae*) released near his camp to obtain some idea of the natural diet of this species. He suggested that leaves from two species of vine (both *Scaveola* spp.) and fronds from an epiphytic Bird's Nest Fern (*Asplenium*) were important food items.

Will Betz, from the University of Southhampton, and Lisa Dabek, from Roger Williams Park Zoo on Rhode Island, conducted extensive interviews with hunters to obtain information about the food plants of Matschie's (*D. matschiei*), Goodfellow's (*D. goodfellowi buergersi*) and Doria's (*D. dorianus notatus*) Tree-kangaroos. They did this in Morobe Province on the Huon Peninsula (for Matschie's Tree-kangaroo) and in the Crater Mountains Wildlife Management Area in the Eastern Highlands (for Goodfellow's and Doria's).

They were able to identify 91 food plants from the Huon site and a further 70 from Crater Mountain. Overall, their plant lists suggest that the tree-kangaroos in both areas were particularly partial to ferns, and ferns from six families (Aspleniaceae, Blechnaceae, Cyatheaceae, Dryopteridaceae, Marratia and Polypodiaceae) were identified as food plants. Various species of *Marratia*, which are large terrestrial ferns that grow in the mid-montane forests, were identified as tree-kangaroo food plants by every group of hunters they spoke to, as was the river bank herb *Impatiens hawkeri* (Balsaminaceae). Climbing Pandans (*Freycinetia* sp. from the genus Pandanaceae), gingers (Zingiberaceae), vines and shrubs from the genus *Rubus* (Rosaceae), and trees from the genus *Timonius* (Rubiaceae) were also significant.

One apparent difference in food preference between the two areas was in the use of epiphytic orchids (Orchidaceae). Several species were identified as food plants by landowners on the Huon whereas the Eastern Highlanders didn't identify any orchids that were eaten by tree-kangaroos. The Huon hunters also delineated which parts of the plants were being eaten, and indicated that Matschie's Tree-kangaroo preferred the stems and young leaves and rarely had the fruit or flowers in its diet.

Carnivory

Many tree-kangaroos are held in zoos and the diets fed to them can provide some insights into the range of foods they eat. Because adequate protein intake is always a concern with captive animals, boiled eggs, mealworms and even day-old chickens are often fed. In one German zoo Goodfellow's Tree-kanga-roos (*D. goodfellow buergersi*) were fed live chickens and although those responsible for their husbandry argued that it helped keep the tree-kangaroos in good health, it is a controversial practice.

But there are reports of active carnivory by captive tree-kangaroos. Judie Steenberg, from Woodland Park Zoo in Seattle, reported one of their Matschie's Tree-kangaroos hunting down and partially eating a Nicobar Pigeon that had been released into the enclosure a short time earlier. Peter Johnson, Mark Hawkes and Scott Sullivan from the Queensland National Parks Captive Breeding Centre at Townsville have observed numerous acts of carnivory by their captive Lumholtz's Tree-kangaroos. One morning they witnessed an adult male breakfasting on a freshly killed 1.2 metre Carpet Python (*Morelia spilota*). They often see the tree-kangaroos chasing Peaceful Doves (*Geopelia striata*) around the enclosure and once observed a male catch and then consume the brain and breast muscle of one unfortunate bird. Hatchling Australian Brush Turkeys (*Alectura lathami*) that occasionally wander into the tree-kangaroo enclosure are also killed and have their brains eaten.

These observations lead one to speculate whether carnivory by tree-kangaroos is an artefact of captivity, driven by dietary deficiency or boredom, or indicative of their true nature. In the rainforest canopy wild tree-kangaroos must come across plenty of opportunities to partake of meat. Bird's nests, with freshly hatched young in them, must be frequently encountered. Do they eat them? So far, there isn't any evidence to suggest they do – but many students of tree-kangaroos (myself included) wouldn't be at all surprised if they did.

Diet of Australian tree-kangaroos

With the exception of hunter interviews, the information on the feeding preferences of New Guinea tree-kangaroos is largely based on observations of captive animals or on incidental observations of wild animals by collectors and naturalists. Information from such sources has its shortcomings. Even the information gained from interviews with New Guinea hunters, as valuable as it is, has to be treated with a little caution. Traditional natural history knowledge always incorporates some cultural and spiritual beliefs and, without excellent language skills, it is often hard to sift these from the biological facts.

Observational studies of free-living animals by trained scientists provide more reliable information and when it comes to the diet of wild tree-kangaroos, most effort has been directed at studying the two Australian species.

Lumholtz's Tree-kangaroo

Liz Proctor-Grey, a graduate student from Harvard University, pioneered ecological field research on tree-kangaroos when she studied a wild population of Lumholtz's Tree-kangaroo in the Curtain Fig forest on the Atherton Tablelands in North Queensland.

The 75 feeding observations that she obtained seems a meagre result for 18 months in the field but these animals are very difficult to observe, particularly at night when they are feeding high up in the rainforest canopy and obscured by foliage.

Proctor-Grey found her study animals to be completely herbivorous and recorded them feeding on a total of 30 species of plants from 21 different families. Of these 30 species, 21 were trees, six were vines, two were shrubs and one was an epiphytic fern. If nothing else, her observations demonstrate that Lumholtz's Tree-kangaroo is a generalist herbivore. Her hard-won data is reproduced in Table 4.1.

In most of Proctor-Grey's observations the animals were feeding on mature leaves. There were four exceptions to this: two of animals eating flowers (of the Black Bean Tree, *Castanospermum australe,* and the Pepperberry Tree, *Hippocratea macrantha*) and another two of animals eating young leaf (from a Deciduous Fig, *Ficus superba*, and a Northern Tamarind, *Diploglottis diphyllostegia*).

Another technique used in scientific studies of the diet of wild tree-kangaroos is to microscopically examine their dung and identify the plants ingested from the fragments of leaf that remain. Katie Jones, from David Chrisophel's lab at the University of Adelaide, used this technique at Massey Creek near Ravenshoe. This site is about 100 metres higher in elevation than the Curtain Fig site and supports a different type of rainforest. Katie Jones was able to add another seven species (see Table 4.1) to the list of known food plants of Lumholtz's Tree-kangaroo.

Sometimes observations are made of tree-kangaroos feeding on foliage that you wouldn't expect a mammalian herbivore to find particularly palatable. Liz Proctor-Grey recorded one of her study animals feeding on Australia's worst weed, *Lantana camara*, which is poisonous to most mammals. She had another observation of an animal feeding on the foliage of the Shining Stinging Tree, *Dendrocnide photinophylla*. Other scientists studying Lumholtz's have recorded equally bizarre food preferences; for example, Graeme Newell, from the CSIRO's Tropical Forest Research Centre, found evidence of his study animals eating leaf from the toxic wild tobacco plant (*Solanum mauritianum*).

Other useful observations on tree-kangaroo food plants come from animal carers. Surviving pouch-young of adult female Lumholtz's Tree-kangaroos that

Table 4.1 Food plants and the parts of the plant eaten by Lumholtz's Tree-kangaroos at Curtain Fig (based on Proctor-Grey 1985) and at Massey Creek (based on Jones 2001)

Family	Species	Life form	Parts eaten
Curtain Fig			
Anacardiaceae	*Euroschinus falcata*	Tree	Leaves
Apocynaceae	*Alstonia scholaris*	Tree	Leaves
Apocynaceae	*Neisosperma poweri*	Tree	Leaves
Convolvulaceae	*Ipomoea* sp.	Vine	Leaves
Curcurbitaceae	*Trichosanthes* sp.	Vine	Leaves
Elaeagnaceae	*Elaeagnus triflora*	Vine	Leaves
Euphorbiaceae	*Mallotus repandus*	Climbing shrub	Leaves
Fabaceae	*Castanospermum australe*	Tree	Flowers
Hippocrateaceae	*Hippocratea macrantha*	Tree	Leaves
Lauraceae	*Cryptocarya hypospoidia*	Tree	Leaves and flowers
Lauraceae	*Cryptocarya triplinervis*	Tree	Leaves
Lauraceae	*Endiandra pubens*	Tree	Leaves
Lauraceae	*Litsea leefeana*	Tree	Leaves
Meliaceae	*Dysoxylum pettigrewianum*	Tree	Leaves
Meliaceae	*Pseudocarapa nitidula*	Tree	Leaves
Moraceae	*Ficus superba*	Tree	Young leaves
Moraceae	*Maclura cochinchinensis*	Vine	Leaves
Myristicaceae	*Myristica insipida*	Tree	Leaves
Myrtaceae	*Syzygium cormiflora*	Tree	Leaves
Nyctaginaceae	*Pisonia aculeata*	Vine	Leaves
Piperaceae	*Piper rothiana*	Vine	Leaves
Polypodiaceae	*Platycerium superbum*	Fern/Epiphyte	Fronds
Sapindaceae	*Arytera divaricata*	Tree	Leaves
Sapindaceae	*Diploglottis diphyllostegia*	Tree	Young leaves
Sapotaceae	*Planchonella obovoidea*	Tree	Leaves
Sterculiaceae	*Argyrodendron peralatum*	Tree	Leaves
Sterculiaceae	*Franciscodendron laurifolia*	Tree	Leaves
Urticaceae	*Dendrocnide photinophylla*	Tree	Leaves
Verbenaceae	*Lantana camara*	Shrub	Leaves
Verbenaceae	*Premna acuminata*	Tree	Leaves
Massey Creek			
Araliaceae	*Polyscias elegans*	Tree	Leaves
Balanopaceae	*Balanops australiana*	Tree	Leaves
Lauraceae	*Beilschmiedia tooram*	Tree	Leaves
Lauraceae	*Endiandra monothyra*	Tree	Leaves
Icacinaceae	*Irvingbaileya australis*	Tree	Leaves
Vitaceae	*Ripogonum album*	Vine	Leaves
Xanthophylaceae	*Xanthophyllum octandrum*	Tree	Leaves

are killed on the roads in the Atherton Tablelands are often hand-raised by local carers. They aim to release them back into the wild and weaning them onto a wild diet is often the most difficult part of the process. One method used is to offer them foliage from a range of plants and let them make their own selection. The plants listed in Table 4.2 are ones for which some hand-raised Lumholtz's have developed a strong preference.

Table 4.2 Plants selected and eaten by hand-raised Lumholtz's tree-kangaroos (unpublished observations by Margit Chianelli)

Family	Species	Life form	Parts eaten
Asclepidiadaceae	*Hoya pottsii*	Vine	Leaves
Balanopheraceae	*Balanops australiana*	Tree	Leaves
Lauraceae	*Neolitsea dealbata*	Tree	Leaves, flowers
Mysinaceae	*Maesa dependens*	Tree	Leaves
Oleaceae	*Chionanthus ramiflora*	Tree	Leaves
Oleaceae	*Olea paniculata*	Tree	Leaves
Rhamnaceae	*Alphitonia petriei*	Tree	Leaves
Sapindaceae	*Castanospora alphandii*	Tree	–

Bennett's Tree-kangaroo

Another comprehensive list of food plants eaten by a wild tree-kangaroo species comes from my own study of Bennett's Tree-kangaroo in the Shipton's Flat area of north Queensland. Initially I had planned to directly observe which plants and plant parts these tree-kangaroos were eating but I soon began to appreciate the difficulties that Liz Proctor-Grey had faced. Bennett's Tree-kangaroos also forage at night and I had to use a spotlight to observe them. Being extremely shy animals, they never habituated to my presence and simply froze whenever I shone the light on them. Even when I used a red filter (red light is supposed to be less disturbing to nocturnal mammals) they still just sat there, staring back at me.

The other problem was that because the vines and epiphytes are so prolific I could not infer that these tree-kangaroos were feeding on the foliage of the tree in which they were sitting. I identified six different species of vine in the canopy of one particular tree and, on average, there were three vine species in every tree they used. I had to resort to other methods to collect information on what these animals were eating.

I routinely searched the forest floor directly below feeding animals to look for clues as to what they were feeding on. Sometimes they dropped partially

Table 4.3 Food plants and the parts of the plant eaten by Bennett's Tree-kangaroo at Shipton's Flat (Martin 1992).

Family	Species	Life form	Parts eaten
Apocynaceae	*Parsonsia sp.*	Vine	Young leaves
Araliaceae	*Polyscias elegans*	Tree	Leaves
Araliaceae	*Schefflera actinophylla*	Tree*	Leaves
Asclepoidaceae	?	Vine	Leaves
Celastraceae	*Hippocratea barbata*	Vine	Leaves
Celastraceae	*Salacia disepala*	Vine	Leaves
Ebenaceae	*Diospyros herbecarpa*	Tree	Leaves
Fabaceae	*Austrosteenisia blackii*	Vine	Young leaves
Lauraceae	*Cryptocarya triplinervis*	Tree	Leaves
Meliaceae	*Dysoxylum sp.*	Tree	Leaves
Meliaceae	*Anthocarapa nitidulla*	Tree	Young leaves
Mimosaceae	*Etada phaseoloides*	Vine	Young leaves
Moraceae	*Ficus variegata*	Tree	Fruit (unripe)
Moraceae	*Trophis scandens*	Vine	Young leaves
Nyctaginaceae	*Pisonia aculeata*	Vine	Leaves
Oleaceae	*Chionanthus ramiflorus*	Tree	Fruit (unripe)
oleaceae	*Jasminium didymum*	Vine	Leaves
Oleaceae	*Olea paniculata*	Tree	Fruit (ripe)
Pittosporaceae	*Bursaria tenuifolia*	Tree	Leaves
Polypodiaceae	*Platycerium hilli*	Fern/Epiphyte	Fronds
Polypodiaceae	*Pyrrosia longifolia*	Fern/Epiphyte	Fronds
Ranunculaceae	*Clematis glycinoides*	Vine	Young leaves
Rhamnaceae	?	Vine	Leaves
Rhizophoraceae	*Carallia brachiata*	Tree	Leaves
Rubiaceae	*Aidia cochinchinensis*	Tree	Leaves
Rubiaceae	*Nauclea orientalis*	Tree	Leaf petioles
Rutaceae	*Geijera salicifolia*	Tree	Young leaves
Sapindaceae	*Ganophyllum falcatum*	Tree	Leaves, flowers
Sapindaceae	*Dimocarpus australianus*	Tree	Fruit (ripe)
Urticaceae	*Pipturus argenteus*	Tree	Leaves
Verbenaceae	*Viticipremna queenslandica*	Tree	Leaves
Verbenaceae	*Premna dallachyana*	Tree	Leaves
Vitaceae	*Cissus oblonga*	Vine	Young leaves

*While listed here as a 'tree', *Schefflera actinophylla*, or the Queensland Umbrella Tree, often adopts an epiphytic habit and grows on other trees in thick rainforest.
?: identification uncertain

eaten leaves. Fresh faeces were also examined for any remains of fruit (particularly seeds). Because of the vine problem, I resorted to climbing up to the site in the canopy where an animal had been seen the previous night and examining the surrounding foliage for any evidence of feeding activity. As well as providing some exhilarating views of the canopy, this technique was particularly productive. It proved relatively easy to see which particular leaves from the many vine species present had been nibbled on.

My eventual food plants list for Bennett's Tree-kangaroo included 33 species from 23 plant families; 19 were trees, 12 were vines and there were two epiphytic ferns. In comparison with Proctor-Grey's animals, Bennett's Tree-kangaroo ate more vine leaves, particularly the young foliage, and fruit from several species.

My list is more extensive than Liz Proctor-Grey's, largely because I studied tree-kangaroos in more than one forest type. I also made more extensive use of radio-collars, a technology that was still in its infancy at the time of her study. These allowed me to keep in touch with individual animals for months on end and compile an almost daily log of what they were eating. The usage of most of the species listed in Table 4.3 varied between animals, between forest types, between seasons and between years. However, some tree and vine species were repeatedly visited and were obviously important to the tree-kangaroos, so I will discuss them at some length.

The foliage of tree *Ganophyllum falcatum* was beloved by tree-kangaroos at most of my study sites. The trees were a beacon for them and most trunks were covered with the signature scratch marks of tree-kangaroos. Its leaves are soft and highly palatable, with a slightly nutty flavour. None of the trees was the province of a single animal and all tended to be regularly visited by the males and females living in a particular forest patch.

Ganophyllum falcatum is a member of the Sapindaceae, a plant family that includes those delicious fruiting trees of Asia, the litchi, the longan and the rambutan. Its own fruit is very small but it is exceptionally sweet and savoured by the Aboriginal people. The fruit is possibly eaten by tree-kangaroos as well but I only witnessed them feeding on its leaves and flowers. Largely because of the quality of its timber, *G. falcatum* has been given common names such as Scaly Bark Ash and Daintree Hickory in Australia, but it is widely distributed in New Guinea and South-East Asia where its value as a hardwood timber has been appreciated for much longer and so it has other names – lulibas, mangir and tapu are but a few. I was to discover that many of the food plants of Bennett's Tree-kangaroo occurred outside Australia and most of them had a similar Malesian distribution to *Ganophyllum*.

Photo: R. Martin

Complex notophyll vine forest at Shipton's Flat, featuring one of the food trees favoured by Bennett's Tree-kangaroos, *Ganophyllum falcatum*, in the centre of the picture.

Another extremely important food tree around Shipton's Flat was a Rubiaceous plant of uncertain taxonomy. It is listed as *Aidia cochinchinensis* in Table 4.3 but its botanical name has alternated over the years between *A. racemosa* and *Randia cochinchinensis* and it may be a local representative of *A. cochinchinensis*, the type specimen of which was described from Cochin-China (Vietnam) in 1790. Or it may not. It is a small tree, obviously with a Malesian distribution, and it is very common in the lowland forests around Shipton's Flat. The local tree-kangaroos are very fond of it and their feeding activity has left many trees severely defoliated.

Another tree intermittently favoured by tree-kangaroos is the Leichardt, *Nauclea orientalis*. Another Malesian species, this tree is sparsely distributed across northern Australia where it mainly grows in monsoon and gallery forests. Charlie Roberts, my long-term field companion in north Queensland, once made a very interesting observation of how Bennett's Tree-kangaroo feed on this species. The Leichardt is deciduous and normally sheds its leaves in the late dry season (October) in north Queensland. The new leaves erupt a month of so later, in the early wet, and it was at this time that Charlie observed the tree-kangaroos selectively biting off and eating the petiole and discarding the rest of the leaf. African leaf monkeys feed on some trees in tropical dry forests in a similar manner.

The vines *Clematis glycinoides*, *Hippocratea barbata*, *Jasminium didymum* and *Pisonia aculeata* were all favoured by the tree-kangaroos in the Shipton's Flat area. The *Pisonia*, commonly known as Devil's Claw, was the most popular. The tree-kangaroos have to be careful of its thorns but the leaves are very soft, bland tasting and probably highly digestible.

Bennett's Tree-kangaroos also ate fruit from several species. One of their favourites was immature fruit from a native olive, *Chionanthus ramiflorus*. These look like immature garden peas and to me the initial taste was remarkably similar. The aftertaste, however, was vile and stayed on the palate for hours. They are only available in the early part of the dry season but are obviously an important food item as the trunks of most of the native olives in the area were covered with fresh tree-kangaroo scratches at this time.

The Bennett's also fed on another of the native olives, *Olea paniculate,* and one of my animals was particularly fond of the ripe fruit. Other animals fed on ripe figs from the Variegated Fig, *Ficus variegata*, and on the ripe fruit of the Native Longan, *Dimocarpus australianus*. Again, all of these plants have a Malesian distribution.

This recurring theme of a Malesian distribution for most of the important food trees of Bennett's Tree-kangaroo is what first got me wondering about the evolutionary history of tree-kangaroos. But I will take that up later, in Chapter 5, which is wholly devoted to that subject.

Observations of Bennett's Tree-kangaroos feeding in gallery forest

Most of the feeding observations for Bennett's Tree-kangaroo already discussed were made in the notophyll vine forests around Shipton's Flat. However, they also feed in the thin strips of riverine gallery forest that grow along the Annan River and its tributaries. These riverine forests are an eclectic mix of plant communities, with rainforest species dominating the understorey and dry-country species, such as Cooktown Ironwoods (*Erithrophloem polystacea*) and eucalypts, the over-storey. Mount Molloy Box (*Eucalyptus leptophlebra*) and Bloodwood (*E. polycarpa*) are prominent with huge Queensland Blue Gums (*E. tereticornis*) on the lower floodplains. The banks of the river are usually skirted with Water Gums (*Tristaniopsis*) and Salwoods (*Acacia auriculiformes*).

Surprisingly, the 'rainforest-dependant' Bennett's Tree-kangaroo is widespread in this habitat. In the drier sites it relies on foliage from the Queensland Umbrella Plant (*Schefflera actinophylla)* as its staple food. Widely known as an ornamental plant (and as a pest species in the forests of Florida, Hawaii and parts of the Caribbean), north Queensland is its natural home. In the closed forests it usually grows high up in the canopy as an epiphyte, but it is also capable of growing on the ground as a free-standing plant and it usually takes this form in the gallery forests.

Photo: R. Martin

Riverine complex forest of the Annan River. The eucalyptus in the right foreground is a Queensland Blue Gum (*Eucalyptus tereticornis*).

Another species highly favoured by tree-kangaroos living here is *Carallia brachiata*, a small tree known as either the Freshwater Mangrove or Corky Bark. The other members of the plant genus to which it belongs, the Rhizophoraceae, are mainly found in mangroves and they all have a Malesian distribution. As indicated by one of its common names, *C. brachiata* has thick, soft bark and this shows the marks of anything that climbs it. Its trunk is a very good indicator of the presence of tree-kangaroos, as is its canopy, which is usually heavily defoliated.

The most impressive thing about the riverine complex is the vines. The thick woody stems of lianas are common in the notophyll vine forests and their leaves comprise up to 30% of the biomass of the canopy, but you don't expect to see the canopy of a *Eucalyptus/Acacia* forest dominated by vines. But that's how it is in the riverine forest bordering the Annan River. Most of the mature trees have several species of vine draped over them and many of these are important food species for the tree-kangaroos.

The importance of vines to Bennett's Tree-kangaroo

For the tree-kangaroos living in the riverine forest complex, the importance of vines cannot be overrated. In fact, vines are probably the main reason that tree-kangaroos are able to live in this habitat. They satisfy all their needs by providing a means of access to the canopy, dense cover to hide in and nutritious browse.

But before I discuss their value as browse, let me elaborate on how vines provide access to the canopy. In Chapter 3 I described how tree-kangaroos use their forepaws to grip the trunks of trees and their powerful forelimbs to pull themselves upwards when climbing. Unlike koalas, which have needle-sharp claws for the job, tree-kangaroos are not well equipped to climb trees with large, smooth boles (such as eucalypts) and have great deal of difficulty doing so. They are most adept at climbing trees with boles small enough for them to grip with their forepaws. Vines are an ideal size and tree-kangaroos use them extensively, particularly when climbing into large trees, such as the giant Queensland Blue Gums (*E. terreticornis*) that grow on the floodplains. So much so that 'vine-climbing' rather than 'tree-climbing' kangaroos suggests itself as a more apt common name.

The Burny Vine, *Trophis scandens*, so called because its smaller tentacles cause a burn-like welt when dragged across human skin, is particularly prevalent in the riverine areas and adjoining open forest around Shipton's Flat. Its young leaves are highly favoured by tree-kangaroos, particularly in the dry season when it seems to be the main food species being eaten. The young leaves of several other vine species common to this habitat are also eaten, including the Blood Vine (*Austrosteenisia blakeii*), *Parsonsia laceolata*, *Cissus pentaclada* and the extraordinary Matchbox Bean (*Etada phaseoloides*). The Matchbox Bean (or Sea Bean) is one of the world's most widely distributed plant species, largely because the hard and impervious coat on its seeds enable them to survive dispersal across the ocean.

Food quality of leaves

The preference of Bennett's Tree-kangaroo for the leaves from a relatively small number of the hundreds of plant and vine species available to them attracted the interest of William Foley, a zoologist from the School of Botany and Zoology at the Australian National University (Canberra) with a strong interest in marsupial nutrition. He analysed the nutrient concentrations in the leaves of a group of plant species that were favoured by Bennett's and the results are shown in Table 4.4.

For comparative purposes, values for the Queensland Blue Gum, *Eucalyptus tereticornis,* are included in Table 4.4. Although its foliage is relatively low in basic nutrients (such as nitrogen) it is still one of the more nutrient-rich eucalypts and a favoured food plant of the foliage eaters of the dry country, such as Koalas and Brush-tailed Possums. A quick scan of Table 4.4 reveals that most of the leaves being eaten by Bennett's Tree-kangaroo are much better quality food than leaf from this eucalypt. Some are spectacularly so.

For example, Native Longans (*Dimocarpus australianus*) were prolific in the home range of one of my study animals and she often fed on them. With a nitrogen (N) content of just over 2% (around 9% protein) she was wise to do so. Foley's analysis of Scaly Bark Ash (*Ganophyllum falcatum*), probably the most preferred food plant in my study area, shows a spread of N values for individual trees (which might explain why some were more favoured than others) but the highest sampled had an N value of 1.93%, which translates to 8.5% protein. Other preferred food trees, such as Basswood (*Polyscias elegans*), Vitex (*Premna dallachyana*) and Umbrella Tree (*Schefflera actinophylla*) all showed up well in this analysis. Most vines are also good quality food.

Vines from one favoured feeding site deserve a special mention. Here a Native Ebony tree (*Diospyros herbecarpa*) was densely covered with foliage from five different vine species. Only three of the vine species were identified but the food values for all of them were high, with the best being 2.19% N (around 9.6% protein). One of these vines, *Pisonia aculeata,* was widespread in the study area and highly favoured wherever it occurred. Its young leaves containing around 8% protein (1.84% N) and 27% fibre, making them both nutritious and highly digestible.

Although it would be interesting to compare these values with those obtained from non-preferred trees in the same area, the data suggest that

Table 4.4 Analysis of leaf nutrients for selected food plants of Bennett's Tree-kangaroo (Unpublished data of William Foley, Australian National University)

Family	Species	N	OM	NDF	N (as % OM)
Vines					
Apocynaceae	Parsonsia sp.	1.49	88.6	32.8	1.68
Fabaceae	Austrosteenisia blackii	1.57	91.5	28.6	1.72
Nyctaginaceae	Pisonia aculeata (young)	1.60	87.2	27.2	1.84
Nyctaginaceae	Pisonia aculeata (mature)	1.06	82.9	28.4	1.28
Vitaceae	Cissus oblonga	1.47	89.6	34.4	1.64
?	Vines 1–5 (Tree # 222)	1.42–1.83	82.7–95.4	13–67.7	1.64–2.19
Trees					
Apocynaceae	Alstonia scholaris	1.58	90.4	28.7	1.75
Araliaceae	Polyscias elegans	1.64	93.9	21.5	1.75
Araliaceae	Schefflera actinophylla (2)	1.03, 1.4	91.4	16.1	1.12
Ebenaceae	Diospyros herbecarpa (Tree #222)	0.83	90.2	44.3	0.92
Fabaceae	Castanospermum australe	1.17	94.3	26.1	1.24
Oleaceae	Chionanthus ramiflorus	0.69	97.0	41.0	0.71
Rubiaceae	Aidia cochinchinensis (2)	0.81, 1.14	85.9, 94.0	33.3, 33.4	0.86, 1.33
Rutaceae	Geijera salicifolia	1.12	87.6	32.2	1.28
Sapindaceae	Dimocarpus australianus	1.98	95.1	51.1	2.09
Sapindaceae	Ganophyllum falcatum (4)	1.78,1.56, 0.97, 1.09	89.8, 93.8	48.4, 35.8	1.08, 1.16
Sterculiaceae	Argyrodendron sp.	1.41	92.4	55.0	1.53
Urticaceae	Dendrocnide excelsa	1.02	77.6	22.8	1.31
Verbenaceae	Premna dallachyana (young)	1.46	86.2	15.8	1.70
Verbenaceae	Premna dallachyana (mature)	0.53	88.7	45.5	0.60
Myrtaceae	Eucalyptus tereticornis	1.24	98	39	1.26
Ferns					
Polypodiaceae	Platycerium hilli (young)	1.11	94.7	56.1	1.17
Polypodiaceae	Platycerium hilli (mature)	0.70	93.5	56.4	0.75
Polypodiaceae	Pyrrosia longifolia	0.56	94.0	54.3	0.60

N (nitrogen), OM, (organic matter) and NDF (neutral detergent fibre) are expressed as percentages of dry matter. Nitrogen is considered to be the key nutrient. In plants, most of it is locked up in the amino acids, the basic building blocks of protein, and so the concentration of N is a good indicator of the amount of protein present. For leaf material the amount of protein present is usually about 4.4 times the concentration of N. Protein is essential for growth and development in all animals and is usually a scarce nutrient for herbivorous animals. Organic matter (OM) is the organic fraction of the leaf. Without getting too deeply involved in technicalities, neutral detergent fibre (NDF) is a measure of how fibrous a leaf is and high fibre loosely equates with indigestibility. Unfortunately, there are often lots of phenolic complexes present in the leaves of trees and the NDF value includes these phenolics, so it is not a particularly reliable measure of fibre alone. But it is indicative and leaf that has both high N and a low NDF is usually good food for folivores.

For some species a number of samples were analysed for N alone and for these, the number of samples appears with the species name and all the values are given.

There were five vine species growing in Tree #222. Three of these were *Cissus oblongata, Pisonia aculeata* and *Hippocratea barbata* and the other two species were unidentified. The animals appeared to be feeding on all five species so the range of values for the nutrients for all five has been included.

tree-kangaroos optimise their food choices so as to maximise their intake of scarce nutrients.

Is the abundance of tree-kangaroos related to forest type?

This discussion on diet serves to introduce the subject of the tree-kangaroo carrying capacity of a forest. This is a very important, particularly in areas where there are various interests competing for the use of the forest and decisions have to be made about which patches to preserve for the benefit of tree-kangaroos and other wildlife. At the present time, and probably a lot more so in the future, such critical decisions will need to be made on many patches of forest in both Australia and New Guinea.

From the information we have on tree-kangaroos in Australian forests, it seems that abundance does differ between different types of rainforest. If I can anticipate Chapter 8 for a moment, you can expect to find one female Bennett's Tree-kangaroo for every 7–8 hectares of complex notophyll vine forests in the Shipton's Flat area. A short distance away, in the riverine complex forests along the Annan River, you would expect to find one female per 13 hectares of forest. Superficially, this suggests a substantial difference in the carrying capacity of the two forest types.

However, it's not as simple as this. Further south, on the Atherton Tablelands, Graeme Newell found that some female Lumholtz's Tree-kangaroos occupy less than one hectare of this same type of complex notophyll vine forest. This suggests a substantial difference in carrying capacity between the two sites. Why? Part of the reason no doubt is the difference in body size between the two species. Bennett's are bigger animals (females weigh close to 10 kg compared with Lumholtz's which average 7 kg) and you would expect them to need more space. But the altitude of the site also seems to be significant.

A group of concerned residents from the Atherton Tablelands, 'The Tree-kangaroo and Mammal Group', were the first to notice this. They were worried about their local tree-kangaroo population and set out to answer some basic questions about them, such as where they occurred and how abundant they were at different sites. They began by conducting a questionnaire survey of local residents, asking among other things where they commonly saw tree-kangaroos. They found that the majority of sightings were in and around upland rainforests, particularly the patches growing on fertile, basaltic soils.

John Kanowski, from the Environmental Science Faculty of Griffith University, had a closer look at the relationship between altitude and the abundance of Lumholtz's Tree-kangaroo. He conducted several spotlighting surveys at 40 rainforest sites on and around the Atherton Tablelands, recording the number of foliage-eating marsupials he saw at each site. He found that *D. lumholtzi* were rarest (on average, less than one animal per two hectares of forest) and occurred at only 11 of the 40 sites. Altitude and geology were the best predictors of their presence. At the higher altitude sites (800–1200 metres) tree-kangaroos were almost twice as abundant in forests growing on nutrient-rich basalt soils as they were in forests growing on acid igneous or metamorphic rock substrates.

An unexpected result of this study was the inverse correlation John Kanowski found to exist between tree-kangaroo abundance and rainfall. Most of the tree-kangaroos he encountered were in the drier rainforests on the western margins of the Tablelands with relatively few in the wet forests of the central Tablelands. He was at loss to explain this, the only suggestion he could make was that it might be related to the heavy rainfall leaching away soil nutrients and lowering the quality of the foliage in the wetter forests.

But the abundance of a supposedly rainforest-dependant species in the drier forest communities on the edge of the rainforest proper is a conundrum. Particularly since the same situation occurs with Bennett's Tree-kangaroo. Let me relate an anecdote to illustrate how this first became apparent.

Very few people have ever seen a Bennett's Tree-kangaroo and wildlife buffs in particular, when visiting the forests north of the Daintree River, are very keen to see this rare Australian mammal. Charlie Roberts, from Shipton's Flat, always tries to oblige and over the years he has struggled to find the 'perfect spot' where a sighting of a Bennett's could be guaranteed. A few years ago he found it, and to his, and everyone else's surprise, it wasn't in the rainforest but in very sparse gallery forest on the far western edge of the species' range. In July 2002, in order to see how general this phenomenon was, Charlie, his brother Lewis and I walked a 20 km stretch of this gallery forest searching for tree-kangaroos. We saw 14 in a single day, a previously unheard tally for such a rare animal.

So what is going on? Are Australian tree-kangaroos really more abundant on the drier edges of the rainforest than they are in the rainforest itself? Or are they simply more visible in the open canopy of this drier forest? I will address this question in the next chapter on tree-kangaroo evolution.

Plate 1 Lithograph of Bennett's Tree-kangaroo by J. Smit in the late 19th century.

DENDROLAGUS INUSTUS INUSTUS (Type of D. MAXIMUS Rothschild)

Plate 2 Lithograph of *Dendrolagus inustus inustus* that first appeared in Lord Walter Rothschild and Captain Guy Dollman's taxonomic revision of the genus in 1936.

Plate 3 Lithograph of *Dendrolagus matschiei matschiei* from Rothschild and Dollman's taxonomic revision of the genus in 1936

Trans. Zool. Soc. Vol. XXI Pl. XXXVIII.

DENDROLAGUS GOODFELLOWI SHAWMAYERI (Co-type).

Plate 4 Lithograph of *Dendrolagus goodfellowi shawmayeri* from Rothschild and Dollman's taxonomic revision of the genus in 1936

Plate 5 Lithograph of *Dendrolagus dorianus notatus* from Rothschild and Dollman's taxonomic revision of the genus in 1936

Plate 6   (Top) Photograph of Bennett's Tree-kangaroo showing the black, ventral surface of the tail; (bottom) A male Bennett's Tree-kangaroo, showing scars from fighting with other males.

Plate 7 Finsch's Tree-Kangaroo, *Dendrolagus inustus finschi.*

Plate 8 Tim Flannery with a Scott's Tree-kangaroo, *Dendrolagus scottae*, one of New Guinea's critically endangered tree-kangaroo species.

5
Evolutionary history

At first sight tree-kangaroos really don't bring to mind the large, hopping animals normally associated with the word 'kangaroo'. They are usually sitting in trees and that's not the sort of place you would expect to find a 'real' kangaroo. Their broad face and short, round ears aren't typical of kangaroos either. In fact, their head and face give them more of a bear-like appearance, and it was for this reason the early Dutch zoologists conferred the specific name *ursinus* on the first tree-kangaroos they encountered.

Bears, however, don't have tails and the long tails of tree-kangaroos are one of their most distinctive features. In the canopy, with their tails hanging limply below them, they look more like leaf monkeys than anything else. But they are not monkeys and, on close inspection, you can see that they really do conform to the basic kangaroo body plan and their tails, although not as muscular or as strongly tapered as that of a plains kangaroo, are kangaroo-like (even if they are a little long, rather flaccid and occasionally adorned with a tassel). Their hind limbs, however, are very kangaroo-like and their hind feet, though shorter and broader than most terrestrial kangaroos, are truly 'macro-pods'. In common with the rest of the kangaroo family they lack an opposable first toe and have a greatly enlarged middle (fourth) toe with a long claw attached to it.

These and other anatomical similarities to kangaroos long ago brought zoologists to the conclusion that tree-kangaroos were probably descendent

from a terrestrial ancestor: that they really are 'kangaroos' that become sec-
ondarily adapted for an arboreal existence. So how, and why, did an animal
with a body so beautifully designed for hopping across the plains revert to
living up in the trees? A good question, but before we can attempt to answer
it, we need to look at the evolutionary history of the kangaroo family as a
whole and, to do this, review the vast changes that the Australian continent
has undergone over the past 40 million years or so of its geological history.

Continental drift and climatic change

To summarise millions of years of tumultuous events in a few paragraphs
verges on the foolhardy but, to gain an understanding of why some kangaroos
took to living in the trees, it is necessary to take this path.

At the start of the Miocene epoch, some 23 million years ago, the Australian
continent was much further south than it is now. It was also covered in temperate and subtropical rainforests. The fossil record suggests that these forests weren't all that different in their floristic composition from the temperate
and subtropical rainforests that still cover parts of eastern Australia and New
Guinea today. From the late Miocene (about 18 million years ago), however,
the continent began to dry out. The once extensive rainforests shrunk to small
pockets on the wetter, eastern periphery and much of Australia slowly turned
into savannah woodland. Several factors contributed to this, the major one
being the continent's northward movement into the tropical latitudes.

The cause of this was continental drift. According to this theory the now
great continents of Australia, Antarctica, Africa and South America, and
India were once all part of a single super-continent, Gondwana, that lay to
the south of Australia's present latitude. Eons ago, Gondwana began to break
up and, propelled by convection currents in the Earth's underlying magma,
the pieces, or 'plates', drifted apart to become the new continents. They went
in various directions, with Australia, which was the last piece to break away
from Antarctica, drifting northwards. It has continued to do so for past 40–45
million years, moving through a massive 27° of latitude into its present position abutting the tropics.

This rearrangement of the southern landmasses brought about climatic
changes that exacerbated the dryness of southern Australia. A huge ice cap
formed on Antarctica as it drifted south, removing large amounts of free moisture from the southern atmosphere. As well, the drifting apart of Antarctica
and South America allowed the formation of circumpolar sea currents that
blocked the warm ocean currents from the north. This further cooled and
dried out the southern hemisphere.

A succession of ice ages (at least 20 over the past five million years) accompanied these climatic changes. Sea levels dropped as the ice sheets extended and at times Australia, New Guinea and many of the islands to the north were joined together into one landmass.

Sea levels dropped 120 metres during the most recent of these ice ages (between 25 000 and 15 000 years ago). Dr Nicholas Ray, from the Anthropology and Ecology Department of the University of Geneva, and Dr Jonathan Adams, from the Department of Earth and Environmental Sciences at Wesleyan University in Connecticut, have modelled what a sea-level drop of this magnitude would mean for the exposed landmass and vegetation cover of the continents. Their map of Northern Australia and New Guinea (see below) shows a continuous belt of tropical woodland linking the east coast of Cape York Peninsula to the monsoon forests of the south and north coasts of New Guinea. This same scenario would have occurred many times over the past five million years with the tropical forests of this region being sequentially merged, then isolated onto small islands, then destroyed before emerging again with a new mix of species.

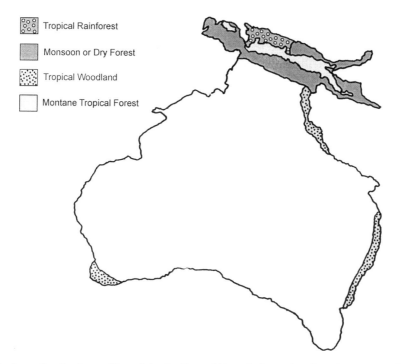

The hypothesised coastline of Australia and New Guinea showing the extent of the tropical forest types 25 000 years ago when sea levels were 120 metres lower than they are today (based on Ray and Adams 2001).

Continental drift and the change in the forests

Alfred Wegener first articulated his theory of continental drift in 1915. At the time professional geologists regarded him as somewhat of an interloper (he was primarily a meteorologist and his original training was in astronomy) and it was 50 years before the theory was accepted. Plant biogeographers were among its first converts, largely because they found the theory to be a more elegant explanation of intercontinental floral distribution patterns than alternative hypotheses, such as 'land bridges' or 'long distance dispersal'.

Prior to the acceptance of the theory of continental drift, most botanists thought the flora of Australia's northern rainforests consisted entirely of Indo-Malay plants that had recently invaded Australia via New Guinea. Now it is generally accepted as being a mixed flora, with some elements derived from ancestral Gondwanan plants and others of Indo-Malay origin. As Bryan Barlow and Bernie Hyland, from the CSIRO's Division of Plant Industry, once put it, these forests are most likely the result of 'refugial surges and contractions' and the 'intermixing of autochthonous [originating where they are found] New Guinea and Australian rainforest floral elements with those of Malesia'.

It was probably around the mid-Miocene (15 million years ago), when the northward moving Australian plate came into close proximity with the eastward moving Sundaland plate (see map below) that this exotic Malesian flora began its inroads into northern Australia and western New Guinea. Fruit-eating bats

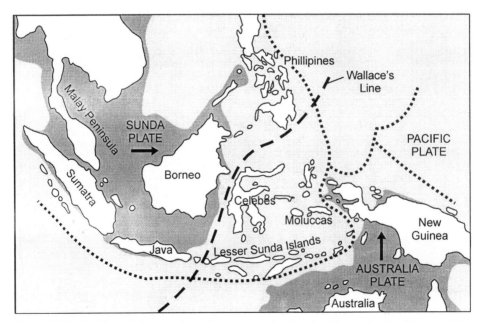

Map of Malesia, New Guinea and northern Australia showing the tectonic plates and the landmasses at a time of maximum glaciation (based on Jacobs 1988).

and birds were probably the main agents of dispersal, transporting seeds from rainforest plants across the now narrow seas that separated Indo-Malaya from the Australia/New Guinea landmass. These plants, which had largely evolved in the monsoonal forests north of the equator, found themselves equally at home in the tropical lowlands south of the equator. And so it was that Wallace's Line, an imaginary line that marks the boundary between the biotas of Laurasia and Gondwana, was breached. Anthropods and numerous bird and bat species crossed the line but leaf-eating mammals, such as langurs (*Presbytis* spp.) and macaques (*Macaca* spp.) didn't and the niches they would normally occupy were left vacant in this transplanted monsoon forest.

Richard Schodde, from the CSIRO's then Division of Wildlife and Ecology, was the first to recognise the wider significance of this Malesian flora in the landscapes of northern Australia and New Guinea. Schodde is something of a rarity in biogeographical research because he had training in both plant and animal taxonomy. He had his insights about the Malesian flora in the early 1970s when he was working in New Guinea with Australia's premier verte- brate ecologist of the time, John Calaby. The two scientists were compiling an inventory of the birds and mammals of the montane rainforests and while doing so they realised that, contrary to their expectations, the fauna groups

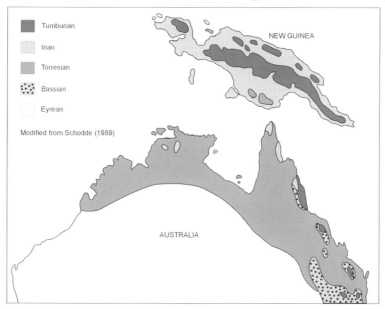

Australia's floral and faunal zones. Modified from Richard Schodde's original map, which only shows the Malesian Elements in the lowlands of New Guinea and in the monsoon rainforests of the far north of Cape York Peninsula (the McIlwraith/Iron Range and the Jardine River). In fact, plants with a broad Malesian distribution dominate the flora of the drier northern and western edges of Queensland's main rainforest belt further south, and this is incorporated in this map.

'had their closest affinities <u>not</u> with those in the tropical rainforests of low-land New Guinea and Cape York Peninsula, but with others further south in Australia, from the Atherton Tablelands southwards'. That is, these montane faunas were 'old, relictual and ancestral' to the bird and mammal fauna that occurred the drier forests of the lowlands. Later workers confirmed that the coastal rainforests of north-eastern Australia and the montane rainforests of New Guinea were indeed remnants of the rainforests of Gondwana.

Schodde's second insight, of much greater importance to this discussion, was that the vertebrate fauna of the lowland Malesian forests of New Guinea was not endemic but almost completely Australian in origin. No one had rec-ognised this before.

Schodde used this information to revise the existing view of how Australia's biota was zoned. Prior to his work, Australia's flora and fauna was divided into five biotic zones with only a single 'Tropical' zone recognised. Schodde divided this zone into two: a 'Tumbunan' (from the Melanesian pidgin word for 'ancestor') element, representing the substantially relict Gondwanan flora of the upland tropical forests, and an 'Irian/Malesian' element, repre-senting the rainforest flora of Malesian origin. He placed this Irian element between the Tumbunan element and the tropical eucalypt woodlands (the original Torresian element). A modified version of Schodde's map appears above and is very important in the discussion of the possible origins of tree kangaroos.

Marsupial evolution since the Miocene

Fossils from a number of sites give us a good idea of the sort of mammals that occupied the mid-Miocene forests of Australia. Not surprisingly, the temper-ate rainforests contained a high proportion of tree-dwelling species. Koalas, cuscus, ringtail possums, gliding possums and a few carnivorous marsupials dominate most of the faunas. Tree-kangaroos are not present, only some early forms of terrestrial macropods. The only other terrestrial species present are those primitive ancestors of the wombats, the diprotodonts.

Tree-kangaroos are presumed to have arisen from a terrestrial ancestor and our understanding of the evolutionary path of terrestrial marsupials from the mid-Miocene onwards owes much to the work of Professor Michael Archer and his colleagues from the University of New South Wales. Their synthesis has been largely inspired by the huge quantity of material unearthed at a single fossil location – Riversleigh – in the Mount Isa region of central Queensland. Now a World Heritage listed site, Riversleigh contains a sequence of marsupial fossils stretching from the late Oligocene/early Miocene right through to the Holocene (a mere 10 000 years ago).

TERTIARY							QUARTERNARY	
Oligocene	Miocene			Pliocene			Pleistocene	Holocene
	Early	Middle	Late	Early	Middle	Late		

23.3 mya   15 mya   5.2 mya   2 mya   10 000 ya   Present

Geological eras in Australia (based on Archer *et al.* 1991).

The macropodid material from the late Oligocene/early Miocene era mainly comprises small, forest dwelling 'rat-kangaroos' that are thought to be the ancestral macropods. Their fossilised teeth indicate that these early kangaroos exploited a range of niches, and dentitions adapted for leaf-eating and for carnivory are both seen. However, kangaroos with high-crowned molars, presumably adapted for grazing on abrasive grasses, dominate the later Pliocene fauna. This has been interpreted to mean that the drying out of the continent and the concomitant spread of the grasslands during the Miocene was an evolutionary opportunity for these macropods.

Among the myriad kangaroo fossils from this era preserved in the Riversleigh limestone, one might expect to find at least one tree-kangaroo ancestor, or at least a kangaroo showing some adaptations for an arboreal life. Unfortunately, nothing that can be attributed to *Dendrolagus* has emerged. It seems that tree-kangaroos weren't around in the Pliocene forests of central Queensland. So where did they come from?

The fossil record for *Dendrolagus*

The main problem with using fossil material to trace the course of evolutionary change in an animal group is the rarity of fossils. The record for any particular lineage is usually sparse and this, unfortunately, is the case with *Dendrolagus*. There are only a few bones and a handful of teeth from five locations. This is a very thin record for a genus that has an evolutionary history stretching over several million years. And there is also the poor state of preservation and the attendant difficulties of identifying some of this material to deal with.

The first fossils attributed to tree-kangaroos come from a Pleistocene (two million years old) deposit in the Wellington Caves of central New South Wales. These aren't the usual teeth or jaws, but ankle bones (the calcaneum and astragalus) and pieces of long bone (tibia) from a hind leg. The describers, Fred Szalay and Tim Flannery, identified the ankle bones as tree-kangaroo solely because of their morphology. They thought that the shape and orientation of the facets on the astragalus would allow the animal to rotate its hind foot and therefore turn the sole of the foot inwards. Tree-kangaroos are the only extant members of the kangaroo family known to possess this ability.

From the size of the tibia, Szalay and Flannery estimated the body weight of the animal to be between 30 and 40 kg, which is smaller than the largest of today's arboreal mammals (wild male Orang Utans can weigh as much as 100 kg), but still very large for a tree dwelling mammal, certainly well outside the weight range of the group as a whole (Orang Utans are exceptional, being very intelligent and very selective about the trees they climb and the branches they swing from). It was probably because of its large size that Szalay and Flannery decided to erect a new genus, *Bohra*, for the fossil animal, rather than assign it to the tree-kangaroo genus *Dendrolagus*. But the evidence that it was a member of the tree-kangaroo lineage is not strong and their comment that 'the functional significance of pedal morphology in *B. paulae* suggests it was at least partially arboreal' is about as far as you can take it.

A few poorly preserved fragments of a premolar tooth from what is thought to be an early Pliocene (4–4.5 million years old) site in the Hunter Valley in New South Wales have also been 'tentatively assigned' to *Dendrolagus*. This identification largely relies on the small buccal (cheek side) cusps on this tooth, a feature is only found in *Dendrolagus* and a few other extinct macropods. The tooth also bears a close resemblance to a better preserved premolar fragment from another site (Hamilton, Victoria) that had also been assigned to *Dendrolagus*. Both premolars were said to 'most closely resemble the P^3 of *Dendrolagus bennettianus* among living macropods'.

One problem with this identification is that all of the other material collected from the Hunter Valley site clearly belonged to a savannah woodland fauna, which isn't consistent with the presence of tree-kangaroos. However, as the deposit was in old river sediment, the describers, Tim Flannery and Michael Archer, raised the possibility that the teeth could have been transported from some distance away, presumably washed down the river from a rainforest area higher up in the catchment.

Hamilton, the other early Pliocene site that yielded a similar premolar tooth to the Hunter Valley specimen, is in western Victoria. The site is overlaid with volcanic basalt, which allowed it to be precisely dated at 4.46 million years old. Much of the material collected from here is attributable to extant rainforest genera such as Rat Kangaroos (*Hypsiprymnodon* sp.), Pademelons (*Thylogale* sp.) and the New Guinea Forest Wallabies (*Dorcopsis* sp.). Fossilised pollen from the site confirms that it was covered with temperate rainforest during the Pliocene. It would have been rather wet and cold, but tree-kangaroos live in similar habitat in the highlands of New Guinea today.

The tooth from Hamilton is the most significant of the fossil material attributed to *Dendrolagus*. The identification of the Hunter Valley tooth is linked to it and, as the Hamilton tooth is the better preserved of the two, the

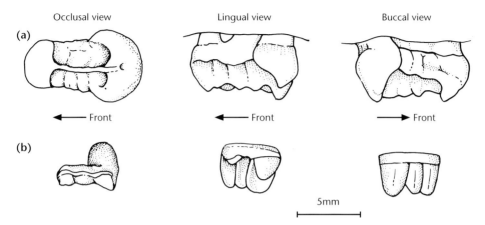

Drawings of (a) the premolar P³ of Bennett's Tree-kangaroo and (b) the fossil tooth from Hamilton, Victoria, that has been tentatively identified as tree-kangaroo.

identification of both as *Dendrolagus* is really dependant on it. If these teeth truly are *Dendrolagus* and tree-kangaroos did occur in the wet-temperate rainforests of south-eastern Australia some 4.7 million years ago, this implies an ancient lineage for the group, possibly a Gondwanan origin. For this reason it is worth having a close look at the material (see figure above).

Without going into a detailed analysis, it's obvious that the Hamilton tooth is significantly smaller (about half the size) than the Bennett's premolar, as well as markedly different in its overall structure. I'll leave it to readers to make up their own minds but I don't think this single tooth is compelling evidence of the presence of tree-kangaroos in the early Pliocene rainforests of south-eastern Australia.

All the other tree-kangaroo fossil material comes from New Guinea. Fossils are exceedingly rare in New Guinea and both of the sites where tree-kangaroo material has been found are cave deposits.

The first of these, Nombe Rockshelter, is at an altitude of 1720 metres in the highlands. As its name suggests, it has been used as a refuge by hunting parties over the millennia and it contains tens of thousands of years of their accumulated debris. Tim Flannery and his colleagues sifted through this and found numerous bones and teeth of tree-kangaroos.

Initially they identified the remains from three species. Two of these, *D. goodfellowi buergersi* and *D. dorianus notatus*, still occur in the surrounding forest but the third, which was represented by lower jaws and a few teeth, was thought to belong to a larger, now-extinct species. It was given the specific name *noibano*. Tim Flannery, however, has since had second thoughts on this and now considers *noibano* to be a larger form of *dorianus*.

A second New Guinea cave deposit, at a much lower altitude (350–600 metres) and much further west, on a plateau on the Bird's Head (Vogelkopt) Peninsula in West Papua, has recently been excavated. The mammalian material has been identified and described by Ken Aplin, from the Western Australian Museum, and Juliette Pasveer, from the University of Groningen in the Netherlands.

The debris in this cave is almost two metres deep with the deepest deposits estimated to be late Pleistocene in age (i.e. between 10 000 and 100 000 years old). Bones and teeth from two different species of tree-kangaroo were found. One was identified as Grizzled Tree-kangaroo (*D. inustus*), the type specimen of which was first collected only a few hundred kilometres south of this cave, at Triton Bay. This material occurred at all levels in the debris whereas bones from the second tree-kangaroo species only occurred in the deepest sediments. Because of 'the characteristic short tibio-fibular contact' of the leg bones the researchers thought that this second species most closely resembled *D. goodfellowi*. This species no longer occurs in this area (the closest surviving population is in the Foja Mountains, which is an isolated range about 900 km to the east). The scientists attributed its demise to the combined effects of climate change and over-hunting.

In summary, the current interpretation of the fossil record for *Dendrolagus*, other than making the weakly supported suggestion that they occurred in temperate rainforests in southern Victoria, doesn't provide any great insights into their evolutionary history. The really big questions, such where tree-kangaroos came from and why their ancestors diverted from their terrestrial path to enter the trees, are not answered.

Early speculations on tree-kangaroo origins

In 1858, while on board a Dutch ship off the north coast of New Guinea, the evolutionary biologist Alfred Russel Wallace had the opportunity to closely examine a pair of captive tree-kangaroos. One theory popular at the time was that tree-kangaroos were a type of kangaroo specially adapted 'to the swampy-half drowned forests of New Guinea', but an astute observer like Wallace wasn't having any of it. He noted that:

> … *unfortunately for it [the theory] the tree-kangaroos are chiefly found in the northern peninsula of New Guinea, which is entirely composed of hills and mountains with very little flat land.*

He went on to make the far more sage observation that:

> *A more probable supposition seems to be that the tree-kangaroo has been modified to enable it to feed on foliage in the vast forests of New*

Guinea, as these form the great natural feature which distinguishes that country from Australia.

In 1887, when describing Bennett's Tree-kangaroo and musing on its possible antecedents, the Reverend Charles De Vis took the idea a little further when he wrote:

Were we to suffer ourselves to be guided by general similarity and a certain resemblance in seating and balancing faculties, we should trace the tree-kangaroo to the rock wallaby, since, superficially considered, the passage from the one into the other may appear of easy accomplishment by insensible degrees.

De Vis went on to dismiss his musings as most unlikely but, over recent decades, molecular studies of relationships within the kangaroo family suggest that the Reverend may have been right on the money.

Many years after De Vis, another museum curator, Alan Ziegler, from the Bishop Museum in Hawaii, also postulated a link between tree-kangaroos and rock-wallabies. He stated that:

The tree-kangaroo genus Dendrolagus *originated within Northern New Guinea when a North Australian land mass macropodid – quite possibly a rock-inhabiting form similar to* Petrogale *– occupied the uplifting area soon after former insular Northern New Guinea merged with this southern land mass.*

This is an interesting hypothesis but unfortunately Ziegler failed to provide any evidence to support it. However, the instincts of museum curators should not be lightly dismissed and Ziegler's statement again raises the possibility of a link between rock-wallabies and tree-kangaroos. Rock-wallabies are a diverse group of macropods (with some 21 described taxa) and there has been a considerable research effort exploring their relationships. Some of this has provided the first hard evidence of an evolutionary link between them and tree-kangaroos.

Clues from molecular biology

Peter Baverstock and his colleagues from the Evolutionary Biology Unit of the South Australian Museum were the first to use molecular techniques to study kangaroo phylogeny. Their approach was to study a single protein, albumin, from a number of different kangaroo species. The rationale underlying this is the more similar their albumin proteins, the more closely related are the host animals.

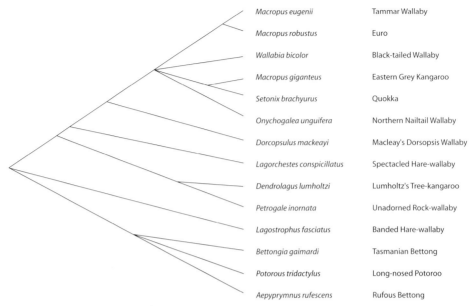

Macropus eugenii	Tammar Wallaby
Macropus robustus	Euro
Wallabia bicolor	Black-tailed Wallaby
Macropus giganteus	Eastern Grey Kangaroo
Setonix brachyurus	Quokka
Onychogalea unguifera	Northern Nailtail Wallaby
Dorcopsulus mackeayi	Macleay's Dorsopsis Wallaby
Lagorchestes conspicillatus	Spectacled Hare-wallaby
Dendrolagus lumholtzi	Lumholtz's Tree-kangaroo
Petrogale inornata	Unadorned Rock-wallaby
Lagostrophus fasciatus	Banded Hare-wallaby
Bettongia gaimardi	Tasmanian Bettong
Potorous tridactylus	Long-nosed Potoroo
Aepyprymnus rufescens	Rufous Bettong

Evolutionary relationships among the macropodid marsupials suggested by the albumin immunological technique of Baverstock _et al._ (1989). The many dotted lines show that not all of the relationships were resolved but the technique did reveal a strong association between rock-wallabies (_Petrogale_ spp.) and tree-kangaroos (_Dendrolagus_ spp.).

The technique first extracts albumin from the blood serum of the group of animals to be studied and then raises antisera to these samples. These antisera are then cross-reacted against each other and a measure of relatedness – called an 'immunologic distance' (ID) – is calculated for each species. What follows is some complex statistics but the end result gives a measure of the degree of similarity between the albumin molecules – and hence the degree of relatedness of the parent species.

Peter Baverstock and his colleagues used albumin from 14 macropod species including one of the Australian species of tree-kangaroo, _D. lumholtzi._ The relationship tree they produced is shown in the diagram above.

The closeness of the relationship between the Unadorned Rock-wallaby (_Petrogale inornata)_ and Lumholtz's Tree-kangaroo (_Dendrolagus lumholtzi_) was entirely unexpected. Some of their data also implied a link between _Dendrolagus_ and one of its closest neighbours in the rainforest – the Pademelon (_Thylogale_ sp.). The authors cautioned, however, that their results were not totally unequivocal and the data could either indicate true phylogenic affinity or relatively slow rates of evolution of the albumin protein in this particular group of macropods. So it seems that not even molecular biology can be relied on to provide the absolute truth, but the results did support what many had already suspected.

Together with Ken Aplin, from the Western Australian Museum, and Steve Donnellan, from the South Australian Museum, Peter Baverstock extended this work and used the ID figures to look at the degree of relatedness of some of the terrestrial fauna shared by New Guinea and Australia. When they compared the Australian tree-kangaroo species *D. lumholtzi* with the New Guinea species *D. dorianus* they found their albumin ID to be very small, which they interpreted as evidence of a very recent radiation in tree-kangaroos.

Assuming a slow and uniform rate of evolutionary change of the albumin molecule, Aplin, Baverstock and Donnellan also used this ID between related taxa as a 'molecular clock' to estimate the geological time elapsed since they had diverged. They estimated that the two main episodes of faunal exchange between Australia and New Guinea occurred 10–12 and 2.7–4.7 million years ago.

Another group of molecular biologists, lead by John Kirsch from the Zoological Museum at the University of Wisconsin, used a different molecular technique, DNA/DNA hybridisation, to study the relationships of tree-kangaroos. Crudely described, this technique relies on bringing together single strands of DNA from different species and then heating them until they separate. The relative amount of heat energy needed to break the chemical bonds holding the hybridised strands together (measured to 0.01°C) is used as a measure of the degree of similarity and hence the relatedness of the two species. Compared with the technique used by Baverstock's team, which only looks at a protein coded for by a limited sequence of genes, DNA/DNA hybridisation enables whole genomes to be compared. Kirsch's hybridisation results supported those of Baverstock's group and again indicated a close association between pademelons (*Thylogale* spp.), rock-wallabies (*Petrogale* spp.) and tree-kangaroos (*Dendrolagus* spp.).

Further work using this technique, much of it carried out by Kirsch's colleagues Antoine Campeau-Peloquin and Francois-Joseph Lapointe from the Department of Biological Science at the University of Montreal, supported the early findings and even suggested a time scale during which the three taxa diverged. Based on Kirsch's earlier estimated rate of 0.44% sequence divergence per million years, the Canadian scientists estimated that *Thylogale*, *Petrogale* and *Dendrolagus* diverged from a common ancestor no later than eight million years ago and that the two latter genera separated off from *Thylogale* about 500 000 years after that.

Modes of speciation

On the basis of the close relatedness between these three taxa and of the various views on how new species emerge, it is interesting to ponder tree-kangaroo origins a little further. When the Reverend Charles De Vis first alluded to their probable relatedness to rock-wallabies and said that 'the passage from the one into the other may appear to be easily accomplished by insensible degrees' he was expressing a gradualist view of evolutionary change. Charles Darwin also favoured gradualism, but how new species emerge, whether it be via gradualism's slow accumulation of incremental changes, or abruptly, via macromutation and the appearance of a 'hopeful monster', is a question that has long troubled evolutionary biologists. (A 'hopeful monster' is a mutant organism that, by chance, may harbour some adaptive advantages.) Today it troubles a much wider audience as the manner in which new forms suddenly appear in the fossil record, without any intermediate forms preceding them, has been widely used by creationists as 'scientific' evidence of spontaneous creation.

In the 1970s, Niles Eldredge from the American Museum of Natural History, and Stephen Jay Gould, from Harvard University, put forward a new model of evolutionary change to supplant gradualism and accommodate the lack of intermediate forms. They called it 'punctuated equilibria'. They postulated that, over the vastness of geological time, most animal lineages are conservative and change little, as the fossil record shows, and that evolutionary change only occurs episodically, during 'events of rapid speciation'.

In a later, popular article on the subject Gould elaborated further on the conditions under which he believed speciation might occur and it is interesting to review questions of tree-kangaroo ancestry and the present distribution of ancestral species with these in mind. Gould points out that most major theories of speciation suggest that new forms emerge in small populations isolated on the edges of ancestral ranges. Not surprisingly, these usually coincide with the edges of ecological tolerance for the ancestral form. Hence, favourable mutations, which would be diluted and spread slowly in large central populations, are more likely to spread rapidly in small, peripheral, isolated populations.

The pattern seen with rock-wallabies, in which peripheral populations appear to have become geographically and reproductively isolated from their source population, fits the classic mode of speciation and is called allopatric ('in another place') speciation. This pattern is not readily apparent with tree-kangaroos, in which the presumed ancestral species (*D. inustus*, *D. bennettianus* and *D. lumholtzi*) appear to be located around the periphery of the overall distribution of the genus whereas the more derived species (the ornate *D. goodfellow/matschiei/spadix* type and the *D. dorianus* complex of species) are concentrated in the centre, the New Guinea highlands.

Colin Groves, from the Australian National University, even postulated a novel mode of speciation for tree-kangaroos, which he called centrifugal, to account for this unusual distribution. However, if we assume that tree-kangaroos arose in the drier lowland forests (as their relationship with rock-wallabies and the current distribution of one of the ancestral species, Bennett's Tree-kangaroo, suggests) before invading the markedly different habitat of the montane forests, then their isolation and speciation there is not really different from the classic model of allopatric speciation. The distribution of the various tree-kangaroo species probably just reflects the geological history of their region.

Integrating the information on tree-kangaroos suggests that the ancestral animals could have diverged from a rock-wallaby ancestor sometime during the late Miocene, possibly in a small patch of closed forest, or more probably on an island somewhere between north-eastern Australia and south-western New Guinea. Isolation, the increasingly aridity of the late Miocene/early Pliocene, together with the arrival of a new flora from Malesia would have provided conditions for the emergence of a new form of kangaroo.

Ken Aplin, from the Western Australian Museum, and Juliette Pasveer, from the Institute of Archaeology at Groningen University in the Netherlands nominate the Bird's Head (Vogelkopt) region of western New Guinea as a source area for many distinctive elements of the New Guinea fauna. Their review of the evidence suggests that the Bird's Head area has been an island for much of its geological history. In this context it is interesting to note that the Vogelkopt Tree-kangaroo (*D. ursinus*) is endemic to this region and that the Grizzled Tree-kangaroo (*D. inustus*) has its broadest distribution there. It is also interesting to note that several stands of evidence suggest that the Grizzled Tree-kangaroo is closest to the ancestral type.

Tree-kangaroo evolution: a hypothetical reconstruction

The question I set out to answer in this chapter was why an animal with a body so beautifully designed for a terrestrial lifestyle should revert to living in the trees. The vertebrate fossil record provided few clues so, following the dictum that 'environmental change drives evolutionary change', I approached the question from the perspective of the vast climatic and vegetation changes that occurred in Australia over the past 25 million years. In this final section I shall attempt to draw all the threads together and put forward a scenario of how I think tree-climbing habits evolved in the kangaroo family.

The fossil record for plants indicates that Australia remained covered in Gondwanan rainforest for millions of years after it broke free from Antarctica. However, with the passage of time, steady northward drift and increasing dryness, a schleromorphic (drought adapted) flora evolved from the hardier elements of the Gondwanan forest. This flora thrived and spread until it covered most of the continent. Only remnants of the Gondwanan rainforests survived, most of them on the continent's wetter, eastern edges.

As the vast Gondwanan forest disappeared, much of its original fauna became extinct. Only a few of its terrestrial marsupials, pademelons (*Thylogale* spp.) for one and rat kangaroos (*Hypsiprymnodon* spp.) for another, lived on in the remnants of rainforest scattered down Australia's east coast. Some small rainforest macropods appear to have adapted to live in the rapidly expanding grasslands and it is from them that the large macropods – the great 'flyers' of the plains that we now regard as the true kangaroos – subsequently emerged. Bipedal hopping gave them a locomotory advantage and contributed significantly to their conquest of the vast, dry landscape.

A few of these smaller macropods appear to have adapted to exploit other niches in the dry landscape. They took to living in and around rocky hillsides (possibly because they were stranded there by the drying up of the Gondwanan forests), exploiting the food, moisture and cover that they found there. The DNA evidence reviewed earlier suggests that this group, the rock-wallabies (*Petrogale* spp.), first split from their rainforest-dwelling ancestor, *Thylogale*, around 7.5 million years ago.

Changes in sea level during this period resulted in frequent connections between the landmasses of present day New Guinea and Australia. From the mid-Miocene significant vegetation changes also occurred. An entirely new flora, one of Indo-Malayan (Malesian) origin, became established in the tropical lowlands, as fruit-eating bats and birds transported the seeds of Malesian plants across the narrow intervening seas and deposited them on the northern edge of the Australian plate.

As they had evolved in the monsoonal tropics just north of the equator, these plants (Richard Schodde's Irian Element of the biota; see figure on p. 67) were pre-adapted to the pronounced seasonality of the tropical lowlands of Australia and New Guinea. They slotted in nicely, becoming an additional botanical element between the most upland forests (the Tumbunan Element) and the dry eucalypt woodlands of the lowlands (the Torresian Element). And it was this that provided an 'evolutionary opportunity' for rock-wallabies, a group of kangaroos that had already developed climbing ability, to head into the trees. They became, in the words of the acclaimed natural writer David Quammen, 'the ineffable tree-kangaroos, doing their clumsy best to fill niches left vacant by missing monkeys'. Such an evolutionary progression probably took place in several phases.

Phase 1: Malesian plants invade the habitat of rock-wallabies, providing a novel and highly nutritious food supply

Rock-wallabies are believed to have evolved in northern Australia. They are widely distributed in the Australian tropics and their rocky habitat overlaps extensively with the monsoon forests. The rock-wallaby's great agility around rocky outcrops readily transfers into trees, as many rock-wallaby researchers have observed, and they often ascend trees to feed on the flowers, fruit and leaves.

The molecular evidence strongly suggests a rock-wallaby ancestor for tree-kangaroos. The two scientists who have conducted the most extensive research on rock-wallabies and their origins, Mark Eldridge and Robert Close, nominate the Proserpine Rock-wallaby (*Petrogale persephone*) as the likely ancestral species. They do so because its karyotype (the arrangement of its chromosomes) is basal to all the extant species of rock-wallaby (all of their karyotypes can be derived from it). This is an interesting choice from the perspective of tree-kangaroo evolution as *P. persephone* is not only the largest of the rock-wallabies but it lives within closed forest and appears to show equal fondness for both rocky outcrops and trees. In fact, its propensity to climb trees is so pronounced that many locals from Airlie Beach and Proserpine, two towns in the small area of coastal north Queensland where relict colonies of *P. persephone* still occur, actually believe it to be a type of tree-kangaroo. In many ways, this animal provides a living example of how similar the lifestyles of rock-wallabies and tree-wallabies really are.

Phase 2: the arrival of the Malesian forest presents an 'evolutionary opportunity' that fosters the emergence of a tree-climbing wallaby

There are several lines of argument in support of this. The first, and perhaps most important, is that in Australia the Malesian forest was empty. With the exception of a few bird and bat species, the animals that normally feed on the leaves and fruit in this type of forest didn't make it across Wallace's Line. So, in its new home, the forest had an impoverished fauna. There would have been many empty niches and, as Schodde observed in the New Guinea lowlands, Australian species appear to have moved into many of them. Rock-wallabies just moved into the niche that would normally have been occupied by leaf-monkeys north of Wallace's Line.

Another Australian denizen of this Malesian forest, the Striped Possum (*Dactylopsila trivirgata*), appears to have done a similar thing and it is interesting to relate what we know of its evolutionary history. First collected by Alfred Russel Wallace on the Aru Islands, the Striped Possum is widespread in the tropical lowlands of Australia and New Guinea. It's a very unusual possum because, unlike most of its kinfolk, it's insectivorous rather than herbivorous. It feeds on a range of insects but its favourite (and highest quality) food is the larvae of wood-boring beetles. These are very fat and a rich food source but, as they are usually deep in the wood of dead trees, they are not easy to get. The Striped Possum has undergone some exquisite adaptations to fit it for the task. It has chisel-like lower incisors that enable it to chew into the wood and expose the underlying tunnels of the larvae and an elongated 4th digit on the forepaw to hook the grubs out.

Among his many accomplishments, the American biologist Jared Diamond is an expert on the avian fauna of Wallacia. He once pointed out that the Striped Possum is really exploiting a vacant bird niche – one that is occupied by woodpeckers in the forests north of Wallace's Line. Fossil material unearthed at Riversleigh has been attributed to *Dactylopsila* and the genus appears to have an Australian origin. There is only one extant species in Australia but there are four in New Guinea and their radiation has largely been in the montane rainforests there. So in many ways, the evolutionary path of striped possums appears analogous to that of tree-kangaroos.

To return to tree-kangaroos, a second compelling reason to regard the arrival of Malesian plants in Australia as an evolutionary opportunity for them is that, compared with the existing schleromorphic flora, these plants provided superior quality food. As I pointed out in the previous chapter, Malesian species are prominent in the diet of Bennett's Tree-kangaroo. Chemical analysis demonstrates that their leaves are highly digestible and an excellent source of basic nutrients for herbivores, certainly much better than eucalypt foliage, which is the staple diet of folivorous marsupials in most parts of Australia.

Phase 3: the ancestral tree-kangaroo disperses throughout the lowland Malesian forest

The tectonic evidence suggests that the southern part of western Papua is a continuation of the Queensland part of the Australian Plate. Once they were a contiguous landmass but sea levels and the extent of the exposed landmass has changed many times over the past five million years. A reconstruction of the situation when sea levels were 120 metres lower than the present day, (see the map opposite) shows a contiguous Cape York Peninsula/southern New Guinea landmass covered with a mixture of monsoon forest, dry forest and tropical woodland.

It's probable that an ancestral species of tree-kangaroo once occupied the monsoon forest throughout this contiguous landmass. The current distribution of the ancestral group of tree-kangaroos (*D. bennettianus*, *D. lumholtzi* and *D. inustus*) is best interpreted as the result of vicariance; that is, a splitting

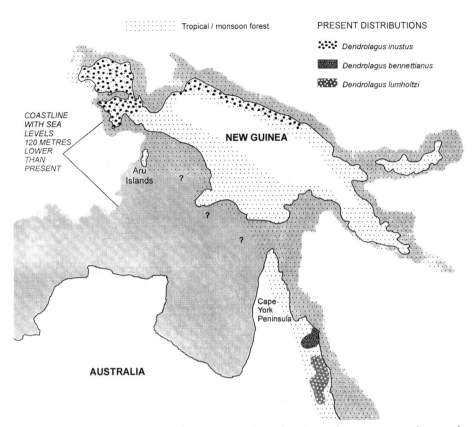

The current distributions of the three ancestral species of tree-kangaroo superimposed over the Australo-New Guinea landmass at a time when sea levels were 120 metres lower than they are today. The extent of the tropical forest/monsoon forest is based on Ray and Adams (2001).

up of the distribution of a single ancestral species by sea level change and the divergence of the isolated populations into three separate species. The genetic evidence of Jocelyn Bowler and Mark Eldridge (summarised in Chapter 2) gives some support to this and suggests *D. inustus* is closest to the basal species. The contiguous band of dry forest and tropical woodland up the eastern Cape York Peninsula and then west along the southern boundary of the high mountain backbone of New Guinea, postulated by Ray and Adams, would explain the unusual distribution pattern of these ancestral species.

Phase 4: tree-kangaroos invade and then speciate in the montane rainforests

Today about half of the described species of tree-kangaroos occur in the highlands of New Guinea and in thinking about this we need to remember that these uplands are geologically very young. The tectonic evidence suggests that most of the uplifting has occurred over the past five million years.

The luxuriant forests of these ever-wet uplands would have presented a bountiful opportunity for the tree-climbing, leaf-eating kangaroos of the lowland forests. And, just as isolation on rocky outcrops encouraged speciation in their rock-loving cousins *Petrogale* in Australia, it seems that time and isolation in the mountaintop forests of New Guinea brought about the extensive speciation we see in the genus *Dendrolagus*.

6
The rainforest canopy: A dangerous world

The botanical richness of the rainforest canopy and the great bounty it offers tree-kangaroos is one aspect of their natural history. But there is no such thing as a free lunch, even for a tree-kangaroo, and rainforests can be very dangerous places. There be dragons? No, not quite, but there be large pythons, which are almost as terrifying, and there be dingoes too. As well, there be *Homo sapiens* and for tree-kangaroos, they are perhaps the most dangerous predator of all.

Although it is extremely unfortunate for the individual animal that is killed by a predator, predation itself is vital to the health of an ecosystem and predators play an important role in regulating the numbers of their prey populations. Mainly they take the old, diseased and infirm but young and naïve animals are also susceptible. In the absence of predators, populations can get out of balance with their resources and increase to the point where they have a harmful effect on their environment. And when populations are overcrowded, disease often takes over as a regulatory mechanism.

The balance between predators and their prey populations is subtle and excessive predation can be just as harmful as none at all. This is particularly evident in many Australian ecosystems where introduced predators have displaced the native ones and radically altered predator–prey relationships. Many native species have been driven to extinction as a result of this imbalance.

Excessive predation is also a problem in some tree-kangaroo populations. In New Guinea, where humans are the main predators, over-hunting has caused the decline of many populations and, in some cases, local extinctions.

Thankfully, over-hunting is not a problem in Australia, nor have exotic predators managed to establish themselves in the northern rainforests. The native predators of tree-kangaroos still persist and it is a rare, and biologically very interesting phenomenon, to still have them operating in an Australian ecosystem.

In this chapter I will consider the downside of living in a rainforest. Once again, most of our detailed knowledge of tree-kangaroos predators comes from studies of Australian species, so most of the examples I use will be Australian. However, there are many parallels in New Guinea and I will discuss the impact of human predation, which is particularly significant there, in some detail.

Predation by pythons

There are four species of python that coexist with tree-kangaroos in the rainforests of north Queensland. Three, being the Carpet, Spotted and Water Pythons, are too small to pose any real threat to them but one, the Amethystine or Scrub Python (*Morelia amethistina*), is a large and capable predator. It likely preys on both Lumholtz's and Bennett's Tree-kangaroos, but my experiences with it are only as a predator of Bennett's. Perhaps the best way to illustrate its impact

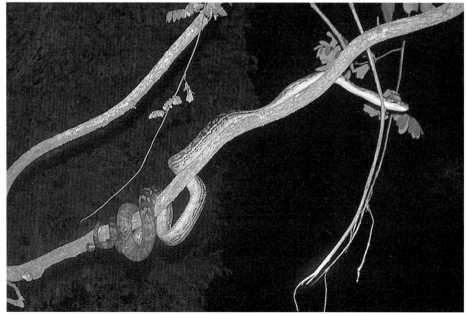

Photo: Dan luby

An Amethystine Python (*Morelia amethistina*).

on tree-kangaroos is to relate the story of one particular python that preyed on my study population.

The story begins in the early wet season (mid-November) of the second year of my Bennett's Tree-kangaroo study at Shipton's Flat. Pythons are particularly active during the wet season and were seen regularly during the nightly spotlighting sessions. Late one night we captured a tree-kangaroo that was feeding low in an Umbrella Tree (*Schefflera actinophylla*). It was an unusual capture because the animal was a juvenile female and, instead of being in the company of its mother, it was with a large, adult male. Adult male Bennett's aren't renowned for their gregariousness and when they consort with females, it's only for one reason. This little female was too young for any sexual activity – at 2.1 kg she was barely weaned – and we assumed that her mother probably had been frightened off when the adult male arrived at the food tree. So we fitted a radio-collar and released the juvenile.

Eleven days later, despite her wanderings in the surrounding forest, she hadn't joined up with an adult female. This was also unusual because in our experience juveniles of similar age had no difficulty finding their mothers if they became separated. We concluded that the mother was no longer around and, given that they usually show great loyalty to their home range, it appeared that she might be dead.

On the morning of the 12th day the juvenile's radio signal was coming from under the dead foliage of a recently fallen tree and she was obviously on the ground. I carefully peered through the debris for a closer look, hoping to be able to recapture her if she was just sitting there in a debilitated condition. Instead I was confronted by what looked like a huge reptilian ball. It was the tree-kangaroo – but inside an engorged Amethystine Python!

The python was lying near an *Aidia cochinchinensis* tree that had a heavily scratched trunk and was obviously a popular food tree for the local tree-kangaroos. Pythons are ambush predators and it had probably been waiting at the base of this tree for several days and taken the young animal when it arrived there the previous night to feed. The python had then moved the short distance to the fallen tree to get out of sight while it digested its kill.

Not wanting the python to regurgitate, we let it lie for a few days. When we eventually pulled it out, it measured 3.3 metres and weighed 10.5 kg, which is about average for an Amethystine (although they are thought to be much larger – the famous Australian herpetologist Eric Worrell once recorded a 8.5 metre giant from the Johnson River gorge). But our python did have a huge head and with it a mouth big enough to swallow a tree-kangaroo.

It also had a long scar across its throat. Pythons sometimes incur damage when they kill prey and this rip looked as though it may have been inflicted by an animal struggling to free itself of the deadly coils. The scar wasn't very fresh so the juvenile probably didn't do it – but the missing adult female may have.

Pythons have a narrow pyloric sphincter and the radio-transmitter ingested with the juvenile tree-kangaroo got stuck in its stomach. Fortunately the transmitter was sealed well enough to survive the python's digestive juices and it kept beeping, which enabled us to keep track of the python for six weeks and gain some valuable insights into its habits, particularly its hunting activities.

A diagram of the track it followed during that time (see map below) shows that the python had three periods of substantial inactivity, each of about eight days duration, when it digested kills. When active, it moved as much as 350 metres each 24 hours but, on average, it moved around 190 metres each day. It spent several weeks in the open eucalyptus forest before re-entering the rainforest where it was sometimes on the ground and sometimes in the canopy.

Shortly after it re-entered the rainforest, and 35 days after it killed the first juvenile, the python moved up into the canopy in the centre of the range of another adult female tree-kangaroo. She was accompanied by a male offspring that disappeared shortly after the python arrived. That juvenile wasn't fitted with a radio-collar but the circumstances of its disappearance indicated that

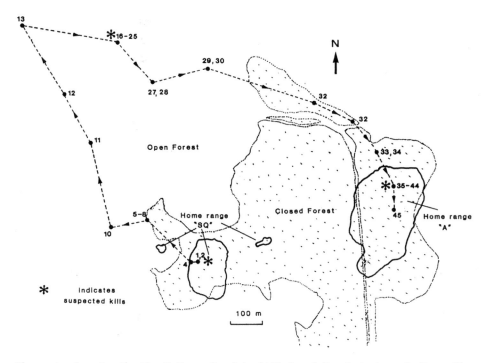

The route of an Amethystine Python after it had killed and digested a juvenile Bennett's Tree-kangaroo.

the python had eaten it. The python stayed in the same position in the canopy, digesting the juvenile, for eight days before it started moving again. Shortly after this we removed it from the study site to recover the radio-transmitter, which was surgically removed from its stomach.

This story illustrates the impact one python can have on a tree-kangaroo population. In a study area that covered 36 hectares and containing about 12 tree-kangaroos, it ate two juvenile animals (which was half of the annual crop of young), and probably an adult female as well, in less than two months. Had it not been removed at the time it was (part way through the wet season, which is the main feeding time for pythons), it may have taken more of the population.

I've always found the directness of its course, into the centre of the range of the second female, uncanny. At the time I speculated if it was purposeful – if the python knew exactly where it was going and why it was going there. And I've often wondered if this gnarled old veteran was something of a tree-kangaroo specialist and went around visiting the females at this time each year, harvesting their young. Elapid snakes follow a routine when they wake from hibernation each year, and visit the same haunts for a feed. Unfortunately, there have been very few field studies of Amethystines and so, for the time being, the mind of this particular python species remains a mystery.

Overall, this vignette of six weeks in the life of an Amethystine Python serves to show that it is a potent predator of tree-kangaroos. In fact, at the present time, they are probably the most significant predator. However, given the current buoyant state of Bennett's Tree-kangaroo populations, it appears to be a relationship that is in balance.

There are also pythons in New Guinea but most are too small to threaten tree-kangaroos. Amethystine Pythons mainly occur in the lowlands but, these days, there aren't very many tree-kangaroos surviving there. On the other hand, Boelen's Python (*Morelia boeleni*) inhabits montane rainforests above 1000 metres and this puts them well within the range of several tree-kangaroo species. Approaching 3 metres in length, they are large enough to take a juvenile tree-kangaroo should they encounter one. And although Western zoologists have yet to confirm it, Olo hunters maintain that there is a large python species living in the Torricelli Mountains that takes tree-kangaroos.

Avian predators

In Australia, the Wedge-tailed Eagle (*Aquila audax*) is another potential predator of tree-kangaroos. In the cooler months of the dry season tree-kangaroos have a habit of sitting out on top of the canopy, basking in the morning sun. In this situation juveniles in particular would be vulnerable to a large avian predator, but there are no records of it happening.

New Guinea Harpy Eagles (*Harpyopsis novaeguinea*) are larger than Wedge-tailed Eagles and, in the lowland forests, are a likely candidate for the role of tree-kangaroo predator. They are reported to take large possums, giant rats and even terrestrial wallabies, so juvenile tree-kangaroos would be well within their size class of prey. Once again, though, there are no reports of them taking tree-kangaroos.

Predation by wild dogs and dingoes

The terms dingo and wild dog tend to be used interchangeably in Australia and there really is little difference between them. Recent research indicates that dingoes actually are a domesticated dog of Indonesian origin that was introduced into Australia within the last 5000 years. Dingoes readily interbreed with domestic dogs and, as a result, in most parts of Australia they contain a substantial component of domestic dog genes and are no longer a pure strain. This is particularly so around human settlements.

Dingoes were ever-present in the rainforests around Shipton's Flat and I often heard them calling at night, but the only evidence I ever saw of them preying on tree-kangaroos was a tree-kangaroo claw in a dingo scat. However, Karl Vernes and Scott Burnett, two biologists who were monitoring the prey of rainforest dingoes, regularly found tree-kangaroo hair in dingo scats. Dingoes are very efficient predators and would probably attempt to kill any tree-kangaroo they caught on the ground. Male tree-kangaroos are the most susceptible, especially during the breeding season when they often fight interlopers to evict them from their territory. The vanquished (mainly the young and the very old) are often driven out into the open country where they would be extremely vulnerable to wild dogs.

Graeme Newell, from the CSIRO's Tropical Forest Research Centre at Atherton, was able to quantify the impact of predation by wild dogs on a population of Lumholtz's Tree-kangaroos that he was studying on the Atherton Tablelands. His study site was an isolated remnant of rainforest on private land and he originally set out to study how the tree-kangaroos were using this habitat. Midway through the study, the landowner decided he needed some more pasture for his cows and began clearing the patch of rainforest. Newell quickly changed his research question to look at the impact this loss of habitat would have on the resident tree-kangaroos. Once their forest was gone he expected them to disperse but found that most continued to live within their substantially treeless home ranges, hiding in the debris and feeding on whatever foliage they could find. Animals with ranges on the edge of cleared areas fared worst and six such animals (half of the study population) eventually died. Wild dogs were directly implicated in the deaths of four of them.

Hunting dogs, which in north Queensland are often only marginally more domesticated than wild dogs, also account for some tree-kangaroo mortality. Pig hunting in the rainforest is a favourite pastime and most hunters use dogs to flush the pigs. They flush the odd tree-kangaroo as well and, while some escape, many are killed. Pig hunters seldom talk about these kills (tree-kangaroos are protected wildlife in Queensland and there are heavy penalties for killing them), so it is hard to assess the extent of their tree-kangaroo 'bycatch'.

In New Guinea there is no question of it being a 'bycatch' because hunting dogs are specifically used to catch tree-kangaroos. In fact, the combination of human and dog, working in tandem, is by far the most lethal predator of tree-kangaroos.

Homo sapiens and hunting

The scientific name *Dendrolagus*, which literally translated means 'arboreal animal that tastes like hare', is particularly apt for the tree-kangaroo genus because so much of its recent history has been shaped by its status as human food. It is our species, *Homo sapiens*, that has been the most significant predator of tree-kangaroo populations in both Australia and New Guinea for much of the past 40 000 years. This predation has had – and still is having – a significant impact on tree-kangaroo populations.

Aboriginal hunting and Lumholtz's Tree-kangaroo

Carl Lumholtz, who collected the first described species of Australian tree-kangaroo in 1881, gives a comprehensive first-hand account of Aboriginal hunting. Lumholtz spent 14 months collecting animals in the Herbert River district of Far North Queensland and for most of this time he was accompanied by local Aboriginal hunters who were still living a traditional lifestyle. It was they who first told him of 'boongary', a creature that 'lived in the highest trees on the summit of the Coast Mountains' that Lumholtz believed it to be a tree-kangaroo and was very anxious to collect. After one of his early trips into the forest he wrote:

> We searched the scrubs in the vicinity thoroughly and found many traces of boongary in the trees but they were all old. The animal had been exterminated by the natives. It could be hunted more easily here, for the reason that the lawyer palm is rare, and consequently the woods are less dense. The natives told me that their 'old men' in former times had killed many boongary in these woods on the tableland.

Eventually, he did find fresh evidence of tree-kangaroos:

The next day we came into a wild region abounding in scrubs and declivities. Progress was most difficult and it was almost impossible to find a suitable place to camp. We remained here several days. I had never before seen so many fresh traces of boongary and the natives did their best to secure specimens of the animal in this terrible locality; but we had no dog, for the tribes we had visited had none, and the want of dogs was a great misfortune.

It was only after three months of unsuccessful searching that Lumholtz recruited a hunter with a good dog and collected his first tree-kangaroo. He describes the hunt:

The chase begins early in the morning, while the scent of the boongary's footprints is still fresh on the ground. The dog takes his time, stops now and then and examines the ground carefully with his nose. Its master keeps continually urging it on. If the dog finds the scent it will pursue it to the tree which the animal has climbed. Then some of the natives climb the surrounding trees to keep it from escaping, while another person, armed with a stick, ascends the tree where the animal is. He either seizes the animal by the tail and crushes its head with the stick or he compels it to jump down, where the dingo stands ready to kill it.

Carl Lumholtz's account leaves little doubt that at the beginning of European settlement tree-kangaroos were sparsely distributed in the more accessible forests of the Herbert River district and that he believed this to be a direct result of Aboriginal hunting. They were common only high up in the mountains, in areas not frequented by the Aborigines.

Difficult terrain was one thing that nullified the effectiveness of hunters in the mountains but Lumholtz also suggested that Aborigines were reluctant to go into some areas. They were fearful because they believed monsters and evil spirits lived there. One of these evil spirits, 'only found in the most inaccessible mountain regions' was known as Kvingan. Some of the more remote areas were also a 'no-man's land' between rival tribes. In one such area Lumholtz's saw 'many fresh traces of boongary' but:

the blacks did not feel perfectly safe in this region: mal *[man, especially from a hostile tribe] was not very far away. We could see smoke on the mountains very distinctly, when they burned the grass to hunt the wallaby.*

Further north, on the Atherton Tablelands, low abundance populations of tree-kangaroos seemed to be the norm in the more accessible forests as well. Within seven years of Lumholtz's visit to the Coastal Range, two collectors from the Australian Museum in Sydney, Mr Cairn and Mr Grant, came to the Tablelands looking for tree-kangaroos but only found them to 'frequent very rough country'.

Aboriginal hunting and Bennett's Tree-kangaroo

There is no single contemporary account of the impact of Aboriginal hunting on Bennett's Tree-kangaroo. However, when reports by scientific collectors of the late 19th century, correspondence from early settlers in the Bloomfield River district, and the recollections of long-term residents of the area are pieced together, a very interesting story emerges.

Richard Wolfgang Semon from the University of Jena, a comparative anatomist and protégé of Ernst Haeckel, was the first scientific collector to visit the area, arriving in Cooktown in June 1892. He was particularly interested in the growth and development of marsupial young and initially concentrated his efforts collecting pouch young from the Red Kangaroos (probably *Macropus antilopinus*) that were prolific at that time on the plains inland from Cooktown. However, his brief also included collecting one or two specimens 'of the singular and very rare Queensland tree-kangaroo' whose existence on the Australian continent 'was first recorded 11 years ago by the Norwegian traveller, Carl Lumholtz'.

Semon made some enquiries around Cooktown and heard that tree-kangaroos 'had been lately seen in the tin yielding mountain region at the foot of Mount Finnigan'. So, with a dray loaded with his collecting gear and 'great quantities of alcohol for the preservation of animals' he and his party set out. Upon arrival at the foot of Mount Finnigan they found that they had been misinformed and that tree-kangaroos hadn't been seen there but higher up 'in the dense forest covering its summit'. Apparently the people who had first brought the news of tree-kangaroos to Cooktown were tin miners then living in a camp at 2000 feet (600 metres) elevation on the mountain. So, carrying all of their essential gear, Semon and his party set out on foot 'through densely-entwined forests, over slippery rocks, and through icy mountain streams' to the tin miner's camp.

On reaching it they were disappointed to hear that tree-kangaroos weren't very abundant there either. The four resident miners, 'honest and sober men', told them that in the two years they had been on the mountain they had only seen tree-kangaroos twice. Semon and his party spent several days searching and found fresh dung but, like everyone else who has sought tree-kangaroos, they concluded that 'to hunt the creatures with success a good dog is indispensable,' and that it was useless to continue their search without one. So they left empty-handed, Semon taking home with him only the pleasurable memories of his visit 'to the camp of the tin-diggers and of my tiring excursion in their magnificent forests'.

Two years later Edgar Waite, from the Australian Museum, published a short paper summarising what was then known of Bennett's Tree-kangaroo. His main informant was Robert Hislop, a local resident of the Bloomfield River district. Waite quoted him as saying that:

> the blacks hunt them with dogs and are very fond of the flesh. I have found several down on the flat land but as a rule they seem to be the most numerous on or near the top of the hill ridges here, which are about 1500 to 2500 feet high.

Robert Hislop was probably the most knowledgeable European in the district on the habits of tree-kangaroos. He had been Dudley Le Souef's guide during the two visits he made to the area (in 1893 and 1896) to collect tree-kangaroos. Le Souef, the Assistant Director of Melbourne's Zoological Gardens, was intent on collecting tree-kangaroos for his zoo and travelled widely in the area on his first visit, visiting Cedar Bay, Mount Romeo and the Finlayson Range, as well as the valley of the Annan River. Unlike Semon, Le Souef relied on the Aboriginals to find animals for him and he was very successful, returning to Melbourne with six live tree-kangaroos. He didn't exactly say where he got them other than they were 'found on or near the top of the ranges, where the timber is not so high or difficult to climb'.

On his second visit, Le Souef concentrated his activities further south, around Mount Peter Botte, where he believed tree-kangaroos to be common. On ascending the mountain he saw most evidence of tree-kangaroo activity above 2000 feet (600 metres) and the six Aborigines in his party, with the help of their hunting dog 'Mergo', eventually took five animals. However, despite their belief that tree-kangaroos were even more abundant higher up, Le Souef observed that none of the Aborigines would accompany him to the summit. In an article he wrote years later, he expounded on the reasons why not:

> I had heard various tales about it [Mount Peter Botte] from the natives, such as it being the home of the spirits of their deceased ancestors, also that tree wallabies were plentiful and very tame, but they were only pure imagination as the natives were far too frightened of the supposed spirits even to ascend the mountain, of which they had heard tales from their infancy.

Subsequent evidence on the distribution and abundance of Bennett's Tree-kangaroo in this area comes from the visit of the Archbold Expedition, from the American Museum of Natural History (AMNH), in 1948. This expedition included two eminent mammalogists, Hobart Van Deusen and George Tate and employed several Aboriginal guides. The party spent most of September 1948 collecting around Shipton's Flat and Mount Finnigan but only managed to obtain a single tree-kangaroo specimen. It was collected at the 2800 feet (850 metre) level on Mount Finnigan and it was the highlight of their trip.

A local resident of Shipton's Flat, Mr Jack Roberts, was a key assistant to the Archbold expeditioners. He was a skilled bushman and very knowledgeable about the local wildlife. He continued to collect for the AMNH for many years after this expedition. In November 1949, he added another three Bennett's Tree-kangaroos to their collection – a male and an adult female with a pouch young (AMNH nos. 155114, 155115 and 155150). Again, all were collected on Mount Finnigan.

Jack Roberts had two sons, Lewis and Charlie, who still live at Shipton's Flat and still continue their father's interest in natural history. Both are sharp-eyed, skilled bushmen and their account of the changes in the distribution and abundance of tree-kangaroos that they have witnessed over the past 35 years is a fascinating tale.

Lewis, the older brother, first became aware of tree-kangaroos in the mid-1960s, when he was still a teenager. Until then, despite a childhood spent

Stanley Breeden and Jack Roberts on horseback at Shipton's Flat in the 1960s.

Photo: Lewis Roberts

wandering around in the surrounding forests, he had never seen one. Two visitors from the Queensland Museum, Stanley and Kay Breeden, first aroused his interest. They were intent on photographing all the spectacular flora and fauna of the rainforest for a book they were writing on the Queensland tropics. There were no photographs of Bennett's in existence at the time so they keenly sought a live animal.

The first published colour photograph of Bennett's Tree-kangaroo was taken by Lewis Roberts.

The Breedens spent a considerable amount of time in the forests around Shipton's Flat, usually in the company of Jack Roberts and his sons, but they never saw a tree-kangaroo. And when their book *Tropical Queensland* eventually appeared (in 1970), Bennett's Tree-kangaroo was the only member of Queensland's tropical fauna not represented by a photograph.

Lewis Roberts is a very determined man and with his curiosity aroused, he persisted until eventually, about three months after the Breedens had gone south, he did find a tree-kangaroo (on Mount Walker – about 3 km north-east of Shipton's Flat). Later on, in the mid-1960s, Lewis saw more tree-kangaroos when he started making monthly bird-watching trips up Mount Finnigan. From that time he regarded Mount Finnigan as the stronghold of tree-kangaroos in the area, as his father before him had done.

By the early 1970s, however, both Lewis and Charlie were seeing tree-kangaroos more frequently and often they were in places other than Mount Finnigan. Most were in the closed forests around Shipton's Flat, but a few were out in the adjacent eucalypt woodlands. These latter animals were seen during the dry season (July to October) when the Roberts were mustering cattle. All of them were solitary, usually sitting in an exposed position in a low tree. When Lewis and Charlie captured some, to have a closer look, they found that they were all young males. Lewis even took a photograph of one and, when it appeared in the 1983 edition of *The Australian Museum Complete Book of Australian Mammals*, it was the first colour photograph of Bennett's Tree-kangaroo ever to be published.

This trend of increasing numbers of tree-kangaroos in the lowland forests has continued to the present day. It is particularly evident in the sparse gallery forests that extend out into the dry country on the northern and western edges of the main belt of rainforest. The Roberts brothers still muster cattle in this country and over the past decades they have noted a continuous expansion in both the range and abundance of tree-kangaroos in this area. In July 2002, in the company of Lewis and Charlie, I conducted a survey of tree-kangaroos in the gallery forests of this country. In one day we walked 20 kilometres of dry creek beds and saw 14 tree-kangaroos. This is an extraordinary tally and it would appear that Bennett's Tree-kangaroo are now extremely abundant in this country – perhaps more abundant than they have been for several millennia.

This evident increase in the range and abundance of Bennett's Tree-kangaroo appears to be concurrent with a decline in the hunting activity of the Aboriginal inhabitants of the area (the Gugu Yalangi people). Let me relate their history. Prior to the arrival of Europeans, the Gugu Yalangi lived a nomadic lifestyle, gathering food and hunting game. Their traditional pattern of living continued well into the 20th century, long after European tin miners settled in the Annan River valley (in 1886, which was just before Semon and Le Souef first visited the area). The miners established permanent camps at a number of places (Mount Romeo, Jubilee Creek and Shipton's Flat) and most had groups of Gugu Yalangi living close by. The Aboriginal men did some work around the mines and were rewarded with tobacco and a little food for their labours. In the main, however, they had to rely on bush food to feed themselves and their families and so they continued their traditional lifestyle, hunting game and collecting seasonal foods in the surrounding forests.

This lifestyle was described to me by a Gugu Yalangi elder whom I inter-viewed in 1990 when I was living in the area. He had been born at Shipton's Flat and worked at several of the tin camps when he was a young man. He told me that he and his friends regularly hunted in the area, visiting all the patches of closed forest. Mount Walker was a particularly popular spot. They used dogs to find game, but, as they now had guns, they didn't need to climb into the canopy to catch the tree-kangaroos. One place they didn't hunt, however, was the upper reaches of Mount Finnigan. According to the old man Mount Finnigan was a 'story place'. He called it 'Kangan-buln' and said it was a very dangerous place to go. It seems that, as with some of the peaks visited by Lumholtz and Le Souef, the upper reaches of Mount Finnigan were protected by a myth.

With the decline of tin production in the 1940s and 1950s the Gugu Yalangi camps in the Annan Valley began to break up. Most of the Aboriginal people moved on, first to Cooktown and finally to live in missions managed by the Lutheran Church at Hope Vale and on the Bloomfield River. The latter is now known as the Wujil Wujil Community. With the exception of sporadic visits to fish and to hunt pigs, the Gugu Yalangi have not maintained a permanent presence nor undertaken any substantial hunting activity in the area for the past 60 years.

All these facts suggest that, coincident with a cessation in hunting by the local Aboriginal people, there has been a steady increase in tree-kangaroo abundance in the lowland forests around Mount Finnigan over recent decades. Prior to 1950 Bennett's Tree-kangaroo appears to have been abundant only in higher altitude forests not frequented by hunters. That is, areas where access was difficult (because of the vegetation, climate and terrain) or where hunters were fearful to go because the area was protected by a myth. According to Carl Lumholtz's account, some of these areas would also have been a refuge for tree-kangaroos because of the 'no-man's land' that existed between hostile tribes.

Taken together, all of these accounts suggest that humans were an extremely significant predator of tree-kangaroos in Australia, possibly more significant than all of its other predators combined. But what of New Guinea?

Hunting and trends in abundance among New Guinea tree-kangaroos

Europeans did not penetrate much of New Guinea until the 1950s and many people there were still living a traditional lifestyle, based on gardening and hunting, until fairly late in the 20th century. The New Zealand ethnobiologist Ralph Bulmer and his mammalian biologist colleague Jim Menzies (from the University of Papua New Guinea) were among the first Western scientists to draw attention to the impact that traditional hunting was having on the fauna. In a report published in 1972 they attributed several local extinctions of mammal species in the Kaironk Valley (Madang Province) to over-hunting. What was most interesting about their report was the species that had only recently gone to extinction (for example Forest Wallabies, *Dorcopsis*, and Pademelons, *Thylogale*) were still in the memory of the local people. Tree-kangaroos were not, yet the two scientists found a tree-kangaroo skull in an old cooking shelter and this suggested to them that the local extinction of tree-kangaroos had occurred much earlier than that of the other two macropods. To be lost from human memory, the extinction had to have occurred several human generations earlier.

Graeme George, who managed New Guinea's Baiyer River Sanctuary for a number of years in the late 1970s, also commented on the impact that traditional hunting was having on tree-kangaroo populations in the Central Highlands. By that time the local subspecies of Goodfellow's Tree-kangaroo, the timboyok (*Dendrolagus goodfellowi buergesi*) had declined markedly across its range and even disappeared completely from some areas. Similarly the Central Highlands subspecies of Doria's Tree-kangaroo, the ifola (*D. dorianus notatus*), which tended to occur at higher altitudes and in more remote places than timboyok, also suffered a marked decline.

Tim Flannery tells a similar story about trends in the populations of tree-kangaroos in the Torricelli Mountains. The local Goodfellow's subspecies, the Golden-mantled Tree-kangaroo (*D. goodfellowi pulcherrimus*), is very poorly known but appears to be on the brink of extinction. (Jim and Jean Thomas are currently in the area trying to establish its status but I'll have more to say about their work in Chapter 10.) The tenkile (*D. scottae*) is the most endangered member of the Doria's complex and, with less than 100 animals left in the wild there is great risk of it becoming extinct in the near future. In the early 1990s it was confined to two small areas, in the vicinity of Mount Somoro, totalling less than 40 square kilometres in area.

Tim Flannery recounts how the decline of this species has occurred within the lifetime of a single generation of hunters. Old men, now in their late 70s, recall when the tenkile was commonplace and occurred in the forest close by to their villages. They were so easy to find that these old men boasted of killing many in their heyday. Today, the best hunters from the same villages have to undertake a day's walk up into the mountains to get within the current range of the tenkile and, despite their best efforts, seldom are successful in the hunt.

The status of a West Papuan member of the Doria's complex, the dingiso (*D. mbaiso*) also appears to have suffered as a result of traditional hunting. Tim Flannery gives a compelling illustration of this. Apparently the local inhabitants of the eastern part of the dingiso's range, the Western Dani people, hunt tree-kangaroos relentlessly. Consequently this species is rare throughout their territory. The Moni people, however, who occupy the western part of the dingiso's range, have a belief system that is more sympathetic to coexisting with wildlife. According to Tim Flannery, the dingiso is still common throughout their territory.

Other causes of mortality

Living in the forest canopy, sometimes up to 40 metres above ground level, is inherently dangerous. All arboreal animals experience falls and even tree-kangaroos make mistakes, particularly the young animals. The first journey out of the pouch is hazardous enough for any young macropod, but when the pouch opening is 40 metres above ground level, it is very dangerous.

However, the ability of adult tree-kangaroos to survive rapid exits from the canopy is legend. Robert Hislop spoke of their ability to leap from great heights and some years ago I had a personal experience of the robustness of Bennett's Tree-kangaroo. In order to fit radio-collars on the animals we had to first capture them. The technique we used involved spotlighting for them at night and tranquillising them by firing darts filled with anaesthetic. The anaesthetised animal was caught in a net when it fell but we could only safely use this technique if the animals were less than 15 metres above ground. Capture opportunities were rare and if we saw animals higher than this, which we often did, we usually tried to move them lower into the canopy by rattling nearby vines. One night an animal overreacted to our disturbance and just leapt out into the night. It hit the ground close by with a huge thump and then just bounded off. My companions, Charlie Roberts and Viare Kula, ran after it but it easily outpaced them, obviously untroubled by its leap. I returned to the site the next day with a clinometer to measure the height of the branch that it had jumped from – it was 22 metres above the ground.

For an arboreal animal to leap from such a height is bizarre. But it seems that tree-kangaroos haven't forgotten their terrestrial ancestry and prefer to flee along the ground when confronted by danger. Lumholtz's Tree-kangaroo is well known for this and mammalian biologists who go spotlighting for Lumholtz's will tell you that they hear them, crashing out of the canopy onto the ground, more often than they see them. Such rapid exits probably happen a lot when males are fighting with each other. Male Bennett's Tree-kangaroo are particularly intolerant of each other in the breeding season and fight a great deal. A territorial male will chase an intruder relentlessly, along the ground as well as into the canopy. A harried animal will often just jump to the ground to get away from a pursuer.

When it comes to evading a predator, be it a marsupial leopard (*Thylacoleo* sp.), a human or a python, it's probably not a bad strategy either. But if it's men with dogs then it is a serious mistake. Most tree-kangaroos that are killed by hunting parties in New Guinea are killed by the dogs running them down. And so it was with traditional hunting practice in Australia using dogs. Dogs, in the form of dingoes, have only been part of the equation for less than 5000 years and tree-kangaroos have yet to adapt to them.

7
Parasites, pathogens and other irritations

In the rich growing conditions that prevail in rainforest, few niches are left unoccupied. Every life form tends to have something living on it and much of this fauna is microscopic. Unfortunately parasitologists get very few opportunities to examine tree-kangaroos and our current knowledge of their parasites is meagre. Most, however, appear to be relatively benign. The everpresent *Heterodoxus* lice, which go through their entire life cycle living in the fur of tree-kangaroos (and are therefore ectoparasites) certainly are. Parasites of the internal organs (endoparasites), which often have complex life cycles, and pass through a series of intermediate hosts before ending up in their final tree-kangaroo host are often less so. Some are a serious nuisance whereas others, particularly those that occur in the intestinal tract, live in a symbiotic relationship with their host; that is, they get something from the tree-kangaroo (usually nutrients) and give something back (often the metabolic products they excrete are digested by the tree-kangaroo and form an important source of micronutrients).

So, by and large, this chapter deals with the downside of living in a lush environment. But, parasites and pathogens aside, the rainforest trees themselves can be dangerous. Many harbour irritants and toxins that can cause lesions and harm tree-kangaroos if they are careless about what they feed on. I'll discuss these too, but I'll begin with some of the nastier parasites.

Burkholderia pseudomallei and other pathogens

Burkholderia pseudomallei (formerly known as *Pseudomonas pseudomallei*) is a zoonotic bacterium; that is, it can infect and cause disease in a range of different host species including humans. It usually causes abscesses in internal organs, such as the lungs, liver and spleen in a disease syndrome known as melioidosis. It is best known from the African and Asian tropics where it has a variety of hosts, with pigs and rodents prominent among them. However, it is common throughout the tropical areas of northern Australia as well. It is soil-borne and the most dangerous time for transmission is during the wet season, when temperatures are high and the soil usually saturated.

Melioidosis was first described in tree-kangaroos in 1963 when it was isolated from abscesses in the liver and spleen of a dead animal from a small zoo in Port Moresby. This caused some concern at the time as wild tree-kangaroos are an important source of food in New Guinea and this disease had not previously been diagnosed in humans there. Ingestion of infected meat was thought to be a possible route of human infection.

Melioidosis was first recorded as a pathogen of tree-kangaroos in Australia when it wiped out a research colony of Lumholtz's Tree-kangaroo at the Queensland National Parks and Wildlife Centre at Townsville. It was later found in one of Liz Proctor-Gray's study animals from the Curtain Fig site. Feral pigs are probably its main host and because they are so widespread in the Queensland rainforests, melioidosis has the potential to be a serious problem for free-living tree-kangaroos.

Mycobacterial disease has caused deaths of captive tree-kangaroos in several American zoos. The causative agents are 'atypical' *Mycobacterium* species that are usually transmitted by birds via infected faeces.

Another tiny, faecal-borne organism that holds dangers for tree-kangaroos is the coccidian *Toxoplasma gondi*. Coccidia are parasitic protozoans (Phylum Apicomplexa) and their primary host is the cat – both domestic and feral. Although the parasite causes little harm to them, cats shed copious quantities of the oocytes in their faeces and these can infect and cause a potentially fatal disease (toxoplasmosis) in any animal that ingests them. At this stage it is not known how susceptible tree-kangaroos are but Graeme Newell found *T. gondi* cysts in the lungs of wild Lumholtz's Tree-kangaroo. Marsupials generally are highly susceptible to toxoplasmosis and many parasitologists regard the spreading of the oocytes of *T. gondi* by feral cats as the greatest threat facing Australia's marsupial fauna.

Lice

In common with most arboreal marsupials, tree-kangaroos carry a relatively light load of ectoparasites. Occasionally they pick up a tick or two but their most common ectoparasite by far are lice of the family Boopiidae. Lice are minute, flightless, chewing/biting or sucking insects that spend their entire lives on the skin of a single host. They infest a wide range of bird and mammal hosts and were first observed on a wild Lumholtz Tree-kangaroo by the Swedish scientist Eric Mjoberg in 1913. The lice were a new species which he named *Dendrolagia pygidialis* but, following several taxonomic revisions of the group, they are now known as *Heterodoxus pygidialis*.

Some of the Bennett's Tree-kangaroo's that I captured were sparsely furred, particularly on the inner thighs, and had a mild skin rash in the same area. When I looked closely I could see numerous flea-like creatures darting around in the fur, so I collected some and sent them off to Stephen Barker, Australia's current macropod louse expert, at the University of Queensland for identification. They turned out to be the same *Heterodoxus pygidialis* that had been described many years earlier on Lumholtz's Tree-kangaroo.

Heterodoxus lice are widespread on macropods, particularly rock-wallabies, and each population is usually infested with a single species of louse. In many cases the louse species is unique to that macropod species. Shortly before my tree-kangaroo studies began, Stephen Barker and Robert Close, from Macquarie University, conducted an exhaustive study of the geographic ranges of five species of rock-wallabies and of the 11 species of *Heterodoxus* lice that infested them. They had hoped to gain insights into the evolutionary history of both the rock-wallabies and their lousy consorts but what they actually found was very confusing. A great deal of host switching had occurred, particularly where rock-wallaby species had adjoining distributions, and in some cases 'louse species had expanded their geographical range well beyond the host contact zone to the point where it is unclear which louse species was the original or even the most recent colonizer'.

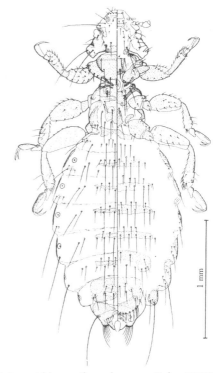

A boopid louse (based on von Keler 1971).

So, as Australia's two species of tree-kangaroo appear to have adjoining distributions (I say 'appear' because we still don't precisely know where their distributions adjoin), it's not all that surprising that they share the same louse species. But it would be interesting to know whose louse it was first, or if this louse is shared with any of their New Guinea cousins, especially the Grizzled Tree-kangaroo.

Roundworms and flat worms

The study of parasitic worms can be fascinating, but it's not for the squeamish as earnest investigation requires much wading around in the guts of dead animals. Ian Beveridge, from the Veterinary School at the University of Melbourne, is one such stalwart and over a long career he has described many novel parasites from Australia's marsupials. The majority of the tree-kangaroo parasites listed in Table 7.1 have been collected, described and named by him.

As Table 7.1 shows, most parasites from the gut of tree-kangaroos are nematodes (roundworms). This is not surprising as nematodes are one of the most abundant life forms on Earth. Almost all animal and plant species harbour a parasitic species or three and their free-living cousins form a significant part of the biota of all marine, freshwater and soil ecosystems. As parasites, they usually form a symbiotic relationship with their hosts and while living and feeding in their gut (and apparently robbing their host of some nutrients), they are often helping digest some of the gut contents and excreting energy-rich compounds, such as lactate, propionate, acetate and succinate, for their host's benefit. So it is a two-way relationship.

You will notice in Table 7.1 that one genus of nematodes, *Cloacina*, is well represented in tree-kangaroos, particularly in the New Guinea species. Taxonomists who describe new life forms often confer scientific names that highlight either what is bizarre or biologically unique about the organism. As this genus occurs exclusively in the stomach of macropod marsupials, the original describer, von Linstow, co-opted the name of the Roman goddess of the toilet for it. Amid the dry scientific prose of a recent publication by Ian Beveridge, in which he describes a plethora of new species of *Cloacina,* there appears an old quatrain dedicated to the goddess. Attributed to Lord Byron, it goes:

O Cloacina, goddess of this place,
Look on thy suppliants with smiling face,
Soft yet cohesive let their offerings flow,
Not rashly swift nor insolently slow.

Now who said scientists lack a sense of humour?

Table 7.1 Intestinal parasites of tree-kangaroos

Tree-kangaroo species	Cestodes (tapeworms)	Nematodes (roundworms)
Dendrolagus bennettianus	*Progamotaenia dendrolagi*	*Labiosimplex dendrolagi*
		Filaroides athertonensis
		Durikainema macropi
		Cosmostrongylus conspectus
Dendrolagus lumholtzi	*Progamotaenia dendrolagi*	*Labiosimplex dendrolagi*
		Filaroides athertonensis
		Zoliolaimus dendrolagi
		Ophidascaris robertsi
		Macropoxyuris sp.
Dendrolagus inustus		*Zoliolaimus niuginiensis*
		Dorsopsinema dendrolagi
		Cloacina cretheis
Dendrolagus goodfellowi		*Zoliolaimus niuginiensis*
		Dorsopsinema dendrolagi
		Cloacina cretheis
Dendrolagus matschiei		*Zoliolaimus niuginiensis*
		Dorsopsinema dendrolagi
		Cloacina cretheis
		Cloacina theope
Dendrolagus dorianus	*Progamotaenia irianensis*	*Zoliolaimus niuginiensis*
	Progamotaenia wallabiae	*Dorsopsinema dendrolagi*
		Cloacina cretheis
		Cloacina theope
		Cloacina cretheis
		Cloacina hecale
		Macropostrongyloides dendrolagi
		Pharyngostronqylus dendrolagi
Dendrolagus mbaiso		*Macropostrongyloides dendrolagi*
		Zoliolaimus niuginiensis
		Dorsopsinema dendrolagi
		Dorsopsinema mbaiso
		Dorsopsinema dendrolagi
		Mbaisonema coronatum
		Cloacina cunctabunda

Table 7.1 continued.

Tree-kangaroo species	Cestodes (tapeworms)	Nematodes (roundworms)
Dendrolagus scottae		*Zoliolaimus niuginiensis*
		Dorsopsinema dendrolagi
		Pharyngostronqylus dendrolagi
		Cloacina cretheis
		Cloacina cretheis

Nematodes

Most of the gastrointestinal nematodes of tree-kangaroos are strongyloids. Mainly these are contents feeders, feeding on the digesta in which they swim, but some, such as *Macropostrongyloides*, attach to the stomach wall and feed on the blood of their host.

Although many tree-kangaroo nematodes have been described, none have been studied in detail, so we have to infer their life cycles from the related (and better studied) strongyloids of domestic animals. The life cycles of most strongyloids are direct and relatively simple. Their eggs are shed with the faeces of the host and after they hatch, the larvae climb up vegetation where, if they are among the fortunate, they are re-ingested by another herbivorous host.

However, unlike terrestrial macropods, which move in a mob and graze (and defecate) over the same patch of grass many times, tree-kangaroos have more hygienic habits and don't come into close proximity with their faeces all that often. Usually they defecate when they are feeding and their faeces mostly fall to the ground under the feed tree. The only possible contact is when the tree-kangaroos descend to the forest floor when they are moving to and from the feed trees. These limited opportunities for re-infection are thought to be the main reason why tree-kangaroos carry such light nematode loads compared with other macropods.

A notable exception to this is the New Guinea species dingiso (*Dendrolagus mbaiso*). Its guts are, in Tim Flannery's words, 'an awesome sight' with 'more than 100 000 worms of various shapes and sizes' writhing around amid the stomach contents. He wasn't the first to notice this because when he interviewed local hunters about the habits of this species he was told that it ate worms! It is the most terrestrial of all of the tree-kangaroo species and therefore the most susceptible to infection by nematode larvae.

Some of the nematodes that infect tree-kangaroos have more complex life cycles than the strongyloids. The filarioids or *Metastrongyloides*, which are often found in the lungs, probably spend part of their life cycle in an intermediate host such as a snail. We can only speculate how they find their way into the tree-kangaroo lungs from there – probably in a surprisingly complex way.

Filarial worms of the family *Oxyurides*, which have biting insects (mosquitoes and tabanid flies) as intermediate hosts, also infect tree-kangaroos. They normally live just under the skin and worms from the genera *Breinlia* and *Pelecitus* (formerly *Dipetalonema*) have been described. The numerous worms that Carl Lumholtz observed in subcutaneous tissue when he was preparing study skins from tree-kangaroos in north Queensland were probably from these genera.

It is not only insects and snails that act as intermediate hosts for parasitic nematodes. In all probability, both Bennett's and Lumholtz's Tree-kangaroos occasionally act as an intermediate host for *Amplicaecum robertsii* (formerly *Ophidascaris robertsii*), an ascaridoid nematode that lives in the gut of large pythons. Some of the evidence is circumstantial but many years ago John Sprent, a pathologist from the University of Queensland, described the life history of *A. robertsii* and how the eggs, when ingested by a mammal, grew into large larval forms in the liver. Sprent identified a larval stage of *A. robertsii* in a Lumholtz's Tree-kangaroo and Hugh Jones, also a parasitologist from the University of Queensland, identified *A. robertsii* in the gut of Amethystine Pythons, who we know are potent predators of Bennett's Tree-kangaroo. No one has yet found evidence of *A. robertsii* living in the organs or tissue of wild Bennett's Tree-kangaroos and thus confirmed it as an intermediate host for the parasite. However, to date parasitologists have had very few opportunities to look.

Cestodes

Three species of tapeworms have been described from tree-kangaroos, all of them from the genus *Progamotaenia*. Little is known about their life cycles but all other members of the group have indirect life cycles and use free-living oribatid mites as intermediate hosts. These mites are mainly found in soil and pasture, which implies that the predominantly arboreal tree-kangaroos must spend at least some time feeding on the ground and ingesting the odd mite.

Other irritations

Green tree ants

Green tree ants (*Oecophylla smaragdina*) are one of the most ubiquitous forms of life in tropical Australia. They are widely regarded as a pest by the human population because of their omnipresence, particularly around houses and in orchards and gardens. As their name suggests, they mainly live in trees, usually in large nests that they build by sticking leaves together with silk from their larvae. They are extremely aggressive and humans usually come into contact with them when they brush up against nests in low lying trees. Their bite isn't particularly painful – but there are just so many of them and they swarm all over you. You tend not to get bitten by one or two ants but by hundreds of them, all at one time.

They are no less of a nuisance to their neighbours in the rainforest and I have seen tree-kangaroos covered with them, probably as a result of brushing up against a nest while climbing into the canopy. We once captured a female that was having a more serious encounter with them. She had large numbers swarming over her, with many in her pouch biting her unfurred pouch young. I'm not sure what the consequences for the young would have been had we not intervened.

Stinging plants

You sometimes get the impression that nothing living in rainforest is benign, particularly when you encounter plants that give you a good sting. The most widely known of these is the Heart-leafed Stinging Tree (*Dendrocnide moroides*) but I have not heard of tree-kangaroos encountering this horror. A close but less virulent relative, the Giant Stinging Tree (*Dendrocnide photinophylla*), doesn't appear to inconvenience tree-kangaroos at all. I have often seen Bennett's Tree-kangaroo climbing around in them and it has even been recorded as a food species for Lumholtz's Tree-kangaroo (see Table 4.1).

However, another tree species growing in lowland rainforest, the Tar or Marking Nut Tree (*Semecarpus australiensis*), does have the ability to harm tree-kangaroos. Also known as the Native Cashew, it is a member of the Anacardiaceae, the same plant family to which the Cashew and Mango trees belong. I first became aware of the sort of damage it could do to tree-kangaroos when capturing one of my female study animals to change a radio-collar that she had been wearing for several months. I had been checking her daily over this time and, as far as I could tell, she was fit and well. However, when I had her in hand and had a close look, I found that she was in a woeful condition. I wrote the following description in a previously published account of the fieldwork (Martin 1996).

The palms of her forepaws were all cracked and bleeding, there were weeping sores on her snout and her eyes were full of pus. She had lost a kilogram in body weight. At first we thought she must have come into contact with the notorious Heart-leafed stinger; cattle that do experience similar damage. However I looked closely at the weeping sores on *her snout and realised that I had recently seen something very similar. It had been in the flesh of my own arm a few weeks earlier. At the time some sulphur-crested cockatoos had been feeding nearby and dislodging fruit. I picked a piece up to have a look. It was a Marking Nut, the fruit of the Tar Tree (*Semecarpus australiensis*). A strange-looking fruit, like a ripe apricot with a green almond-like nut suspended beneath it. The cockies weren't interested in the fruit but were excising the nuts from their capsules. I cut into one to examine it and splashed some milk from it onto my arm. Within minutes I felt like I'd been stung by a wasp and the next day there were pockmarks on my arm as if I'd been splashed by battery acid. At the time I remember marvelling at the constitution of the cockies.*

When I checked my field notes I found that the female tree-kangaroo had been feeding in a Semecarpus *tree five nights earlier. There were a number of vine species growing in this tree and she had visited it many times before. However, this time the fruit was ripe and she must have eaten some of it and got the juice smeared all over her face and forepaws. I dressed her wounds and put ointment in her eyes and she subsequently made a full recovery. A year later I saw another young animal in the same condition and he didn't recover. So, apart from everything else, tree-kangaroos have to be wary of some of the trees as well.*

8
Population density and spatial requirements

A measure of abundance, usually expressed as the number of animals per unit area of habitat, is an important parameter in wildlife science. It's useful for both for comparing the carrying capacity of different types of habitat as well as estimating the total size of a population. The latter is an important piece of information because conservation agencies, such as the International Union for the Conservation of Nature, use population size as one of their main criteria when assessing conservation status.

The converse of population density is the amount of living space used by a single animal. Adequate space is a primary resource for any free-living animal. In an increasingly crowded world, this is also essential information for the conservation of tree-kangaroos because, in the final analysis, they will only survive if they have enough forest to live in.

However, this essential information it is not easily obtained for tree-kangaroos, largely because they are often so sparsely distributed. As well, they are behaviourally cryptic animals; that is, they are extremely wary and hide from those who intrude into their forest. So, if you can't see them, it's not a simple matter to work out how many there are or how much forest each one uses to move around in. One way to overcome this is to fit some sort of device that gives away their position. Usually this is a collar with a small radio-transmitter that emits a signal that can be picked up with a special receiver.

The animal can then be readily located using a directional antenna and, over time, its home range determined. There have been several such radio-tracking studies on tree-kangaroos in Australia.

However, first you need to catch your tree-kangaroo, which is no easy task, particularly in New Guinea. Will Betz, a graduate student from the University of Southampton, relates that in his first five years in New Guinea he spent more than 50 weeks looking for tree-kangaroos and only saw four; two of which were flushed by dogs. He decided he couldn't rely solely on radio-tracking to get information on their abundance.

Dung pellets and distance sampling

Fortunately, tree-kangaroos do leave a few clues of their presence in a forest: scratches on trees are one, dung pellets another. Will Betz looked at the way their dung pellets were dispersed through the forest and decided to use a statistical technique known as 'point transect distance sampling' to estimate the abundance of tree-kangaroos. The mathematical model is quite complex but the data collection is relatively simple and he was able to employ local land-owners to help him.

First, they cut tracks through the forest and then, at marked intervals 15 metres apart, carefully search the ground for fresh dung. The distance from these reference points to any pellets found is carefully measured. Statistics derived from these measurements are then used to estimate the total population of dung pellets in the area of forest being searched. Only fresh dung pellets are counted and as the pellets are estimated to preserve their 'fresh' appearance for three days, the total is divided by three to give a daily rate of pellet production. This figure is further divided by an estimate (from captive studies) of the number of dung pellets produced per day by each tree-kangaroo to give the number of tree-kangaroos defecating in the area.

Will Betz and his local landowner teams did this at four sites. Three were within the range of Matschie's Tree-kangaroo (*D. matschiei*) on the Huon Peninsula (two in the Finisterre Mountains, one in the Cromwell Mountains) and the fourth site was in the Crater Mountain Wildlife Management Area in the Eastern Highlands. Two tree-kangaroo species occur at this site: Doria's (*D. dorianus notatus*) and a subspecies of Goodfellow's (*D. goodfellowi buergersi*). Dung was found at all of the sites but, unfortunately, only the samples collected at the sites in the Finisterre Mountains were numerous enough for the statistical calculations. A density of between 0.6 and 1.4 Matschie's Tree-kangaroos per hectare was estimated to occur in this area.

The dearth of dung in the Crater Mountain Area revealed a major short-coming with this technique. In my work on Bennett's Tree-kangaroo in lowland rainforest in Australia I occasionally collected dung and I was puzzled by how quickly it seemed to disappear. At night there would be copious amounts of dung under a tree that a tree-kangaroo was feeding in but by morning most of it would have gone. When I looked more closely I noted that most of it was being rolled into balls and buried – by dung beetles. Will Betz noticed the same thing and estimated that at the lower altitude sites (below 1500 metres) dung beetles and ants were removing all traces of tree-kangaroo dung within nine hours.

Dung counts have their problems so let's move on to consider the sort of information obtained from radio-tracking studies. But first a few words on terminology.

Terminology

Wildlife biologists use specific technical terms to describe the space that animals use. Two terms in particular are used. One of these is 'home range'. This refers to the amount of space that an animal requires for its normal day-to-day living; that is, the space it normally occupies to satisfy its nutritional and social needs. Often this area is not used exclusively and the home range of one animal may substantially overlap that of its neighbour. Another term, 'territory', is used to describe the space an animal uses exclusively. An animal will actively defend its territory, and drive off any other members of its species who trespass.

Wild animals don't move around their 'space' in an entirely predictable manner and over the years wildlife biologists have tried to develop methods to concisely describe this movement. The earliest and most basic method was to simply present a habitat map with points drawn on it, each point representing a location where the animal had been sighted. However, this was a cumbersome technique and it wasn't easy to make comparisons between animals, so more precise techniques were developed.

The most straightforward of these is to draw the smallest possible polygon that encompasses all of the point locations. The area of this is then expressed as a measure of the animal's home range. This is called the minimum convex polygon method. A serious deficiency with this method is the disproportionate effect that outlying points have on the overall area of the home range. The outlying points are often atypical and usually represent locations where an animal has temporarily strayed outside its normal area of activity.

To minimise the effect these outliers had on home range size, another method was developed. Known as the harmonic mean method, it relies on some arcane statistics to calculate a theoretical mid-point of the dispersion of the point locations. The range of the animal is then diagrammatically

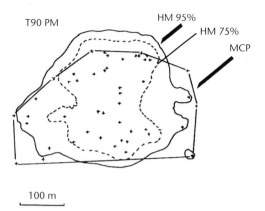

Comparison of three methods of depicting home range. The data are fixes obtained for a female Bennett's Tree-kangaroo ('Tricia') at Shipton's Flat. The small crosses represent 56 nocturnal locations recorded for 'Tricia' between 7 August 1990 and 10 January 1991. The solid outline is the minimum convex polygon (MCP) encompassing all of the locations. The solid line is the 95% isopleth of the harmonic mean (HM), and the dotted line is the 75% isopleth. The area encompassed by each of these is 8.1 hectares, 8.5 hectares and 4.5 hectares, respectively.

represented as a series of contour lines drawn around this theoretical centre of activity (the harmonic mean centre). These lines are known as isopleths (lines of equal value) and the area encompassed by a specific isopleth is a measure of the animal's home range. The 95% isopleth, which represents the area that the animal can be expected to be in 95% of the time, is widely accepted to best represent the animal's normal home range, although some wildlife scientists prefer the 90% or even the 75% isopleth. These various measures of home range are depicted in the accompanying figure.

Use of space by Australian tree-kangaroos

Radio-tracking studies have enabled four estimates of the home range size of Australian tree-kangaroos to be made: two for Lumholtz's Tree-kangaroo, living in complex notophyll vine forest at the Curtain Fig site and some nearby

Table 8.1 Area of the four home ranges of Australian tree-kangaroos

	Males			Females		
	MCP	95% HM	90% HM	MCP	95% HM	90% HM
Lumholtz's Tree-kangaroo						
Proctor-Grey (1985)	4.4 (1)	–	–	1.2–2.6 (3)	–	–
Newell (1999)	1.0–3.4 (6)	–	1.0–3.0 (6)	0.6–2.1 (6)	–	0.3–1.5 (6)
Bennett's Tree-kangaroo						
Martin (1992)	6.4–40.0 (3)	3.8–29.8 (3)	–	6.8–8.3 (2)	5.5–9.8 (2)	–
Martin (1995)	–	–	–	–	10.6–12.7 (2)	–

All units are in hectares. The numbers in brackets are the sample sizes.

MCP, minimum convex polygon; 95% HM, area within the 95% isopleth of the harmonic mean; 90% HM, area encompassed by the 90% isopleth of the harmonic mean.

Data from Proctor-Grey (1985), Newell (1999) and Martin (1992, 1995).

forest on the Atherton Tablelands, and two for Bennett's Tree-kangaroo. One of the Bennett's estimates is also for complex notophyll vine forest, near Shipton's Flat, and the other is for the gallery forests along the Annan River. These are presented in Table 8.1

What the data show is that Bennett's Tree-kangaroos occupy substantially larger areas than their southern cousins. The home ranges of female Bennett's are ten times larger than those of female Lumholtz's Tree-kangaroos, and the ranges of male Bennett's Tree-kangaroo are six times the size of male Lumholtz's.

Why is this so?

The short answer is we don't really know. It may be related to differences in body size. The adult male Bennett's Tree-kangaroos that I captured averaged 13.4 kg body weight and the adult females averaged 9.6 kg, compared with 8.6 kg for the male and 7.1 kg for the female Lumholtz's Tree-kangaroos captured by Graeme Newell at his study site near the Curtain Fig forests. As *D. bennettianus* is about 50% larger than *D. lumholtzi*, you would expect it to require more space to live in.

But it could also be related to differences in habitat quality. Although the Curtain Fig and Shipton's Flat forests appear to be similar, both being complex notophyll vine forests growing on fertile basalt-derived soils, they are in fact very different. Shipton's Flat is in the lowlands, much further north than the Curtain Fig and has a far more monsoonal climate. The average rainfall is greater than at the Curtain Fig (1983 mm compared with 1400 mm), but this rainfall is extremely seasonal. Shipton's Flat gets almost no rain between July and the end of October each year and this is reflected in the many deciduous species in the forest. Such pronounced seasonality and prominence of deciduous trees probably translates to a scarcity of palatable foliage at certain times of the year, particularly the late dry season, which would reduce the carrying capacity of the forest for folivores.

Even so, the ranges used by Lumholtz's Tree-kangaroos are extremely small in comparison with other leaf-eating mammals. Graeme Newell makes this point when he compares them with the Old World *Colobus* and *Presbytis* monkeys. These monkeys occupy a similar leaf-eating niche to tree-kangaroos. With body masses ranging from 4 kg to 18 kg, they are roughly similar in body size, but they occupy home ranges of between 24 and 84 hectares, which are much larger than those of *D. lumholtzi*.

Such a comparison ignores the fact that both African *Colobus* and Asian *Presbytis* monkeys are far more social than tree-kangaroos and move around their range in large troops. To compensate for this Graeme Newell used units of biomass of animal per unit area of range in his comparison with tree-kangaroos. He concluded that Lumholtz's Tree-kangaroo, at 11.4 kg of biomass per hectare, is still on the high side compared with the range of 0.2–17.9 kg per hectare for the leaf-eating monkeys.

A final possible explanation for the small home ranges of Lumholtz's Tree-kangaroo is that the forest around the Curtain Fig is exceptionally high quality tree-kangaroo habitat. Graeme Newell suggested that the carrying capacity of these forests may have been enhanced by past disturbances that encouraged the growth of so-called 'pioneering' species of plants, some of which are highly palatable to tree-kangaroos. This is supported by some other work, but before I go into that, let me describe the successional stages of rainforests.

A patch of rainforest usually contains both primary and secondary forest species. Secondary forest species, also known as pioneering species, only grow in areas where the primary forest has been disturbed and bare ground has been exposed. These species are usually short-lived and, in due course, are replaced by the primary rainforest species. Primary forest is said to be the climax succes-sional stage of a rainforest. (One way to distinguished primary and secondary forest plants is by the size of their seeds. Primary forest species have large and fleshy seeds to sustain early seedling growth in the conditions of low light that prevail beneath the rainforest canopy, whereas the seeds of secondary species, which require bare soil and bright sunshine to germinate, are small, light and easily dispersed.)

Several years ago, Lester Pahl, from James Cook University, and John Winter, from the Queensland National Parks and Wildlife Service, were investigating the impact of the fragmentation of the forests of the Atherton Tablelands on its arboreal mammal fauna and the significance of 'patch size' to the survival of the various species. They were surprised to find that Lumholtz's Tree-kangaroo, the largest of the species they were investigating, was rela-tively insensitive to patch size and lived in quite small patches of rainforest. Originally they were at a loss to explain this but, on reading Liz Proctor-Grey's work, they realised that Lumholtz's Tree-kangaroo eats a high proportion of secondary plant species, such as *Euroschinus falcata*, *Maclura cochinchinensis* and *Elaeagnus triflora*. When they re-examined their data they realised that small patches of forest containing these secondary species were more likely to harbour tree-kangaroos than larger patches of primary rainforest.

So it seems that there is no simple explanation for the different spatial requirements of Australia's two tree-kangaroo species. Perhaps the most important message from this is how hazardous it is to extrapolate findings from one tree-kangaroo species to another. If two relatively similar species such as Lumholtz's and Bennett's have such markedly different spatial require-ments then we must be very cautious in making extrapolations from them to New Guinea tree-kangaroos.

How female Bennett's Tree-kangaroos use their home ranges

While female Lumholtz's and Bennett's Tree-kangaroos have substantially different spatial requirements, both of them appear to occupy home ranges exclusive of other adult females (see figures below). They are not totally selfish, however, and do share their range with their offspring, which can spend as long as two-and-a-half years in the company of their mother.

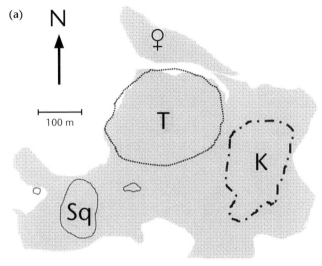

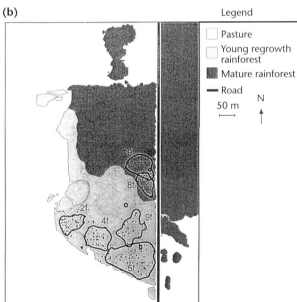

Home range areas used by (a) female Bennett's Tree-kangaroos at Shipton's Flat (represented by the 95% isopleth of the harmonic mean) (based on Martin 1991) and (b) female Lumholtz's Tree-kangaroos at Graeme Newell's study site near Curtain Fig (represented by the 90% isopleth of the harmonic mean) (based on Newell 1999). (a) Both the females 'Tricia' and 'Kiwi' were accompanied by young-at-foot. 'Kiwi' also had another young in her pouch. Only a partial home range is shown for the juvenile female 'Squeely' because she was eaten by a python two weeks after a radio-collar was fitted. Another female, indicated by the symbol ♀, was only seen in the small patch of forest north of 'Tricia's' range, but as she was never captured her range is not delineated.

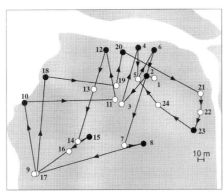

The track of the female Bennett's Tree-kangaroo 'Tricia' between her diurnal roost trees (o) and her nocturnal feeding trees (●) for the month of September 1990. The numbers indicate the sequence of the location fixes, and the lines and arrowheads respectively indicate the shortest distance and general direction of travel between locations.

Graeme Newell didn't report any details of how female Lumholtz's used space but I was curious about this with Bennett's Tree-kangaroo. The track of one of my females for the month of September 1990 is representative and is shown in the figure (left).

During this time the female was closely accompanied by her young, which had only recently emerged from the pouch. The pair spent almost all the daylight hours sitting high in the canopy in what I called 'roost trees'. Located towards the centre of the animal's home range, these were usually old, emergent trees, between 25 and 40 metres high. Typically they were covered in vines and the tree-kangaroos used the lianas of these, which often extended all the way from the canopy to the ground, as 'rope-ladders' to get quick and direct access to the canopy.

The thick cap of vine foliage in the canopy also provided wonderful cover. The female and her offspring were usually completely concealed and nearly impossible to see from the ground. In the winter months they often sat out in the open on top of the canopy, basking in the morning sun, but on the very hot days of the late dry season they usually sat on lower branches under the shade of the foliage.

Each night after dusk the female and her young descended from their roost and moved along the ground to the trees in which they fed. As their track shows, many of these food trees were on the edge of the forest patch in which they lived. Most were small (5–15 metres high) and many were covered with vines. Vine foliage was one of their favourite foods and they revisited the same food trees at regular intervals. At the completion of their night's feeding they always moved back to one of their roosts, but they almost never used the same one on successive nights.

Aggression and territoriality in male Bennet's Tree-kangaroos

With the exception of rock-wallabies and some of the smaller rat-kangaroos, male macropods are usually fairly tolerant of each other. Male tree-kangaroos, however, are different. Robert Hislop was the first to describe just how fierce male Bennett's Tree-kangaroos are towards each other:

The males are very pugnacious, and if two of them be put in an enclo-sure together they will fight until one is killed. They spar with the fore-paws in quite a scientific manner, uttering grunts all the time, till one sees an opportunity of closing with the other, when it makes straight for the back of the neck, and if he succeeds in getting a grip with his teeth, he shakes the other like a dog does a rat.

Male Bennett's appear to be just as belligerent in the wild. The first male tree-kangaroo I ever captured ('Simon') had scars all over his nose, face, neck and shoulders, and his left ear was missing entirely. Initially I was at a loss to explain how he had got into such a state until I remembered Hislop's colourful description. I also read about an earlier one-eared tree-kangaroo that had been captured by the Aboriginal hunters who accompanied Dudley Le Souef up Mount Peter Botte in 1896. He described the incident thus:

The natives brought in two Bennett's Tree-kangaroos they had shot, and one of them, a male, had one of its ears completely bitten off, which the natives said had been done by a Tiger Cat, but the chances are that if a Tiger Cat could manage to chew the ear off it would certainly have to kill the animal first, as the kangaroo would not be likely to sit quietly under the operation.

No, I don't think it would either.

To avoid damage and a large expenditure of energy, male Bennett's Tree-kangaroos need to avoid each other as much as possible. And this is exactly what they do. The figure below shows the situation in my study area at Shipton's

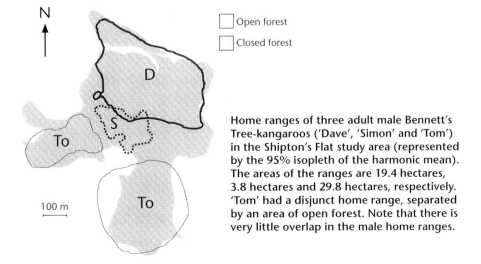

Open forest

Closed forest

Home ranges of three adult male Bennett's Tree-kangaroos ('Dave', 'Simon' and 'Tom') in the Shipton's Flat study area (represented by the 95% isopleth of the harmonic mean). The areas of the ranges are 19.4 hectares, 3.8 hectares and 29.8 hectares, respectively. 'Tom' had a disjunct home range, separated by an area of open forest. Note that there is very little overlap in the male home ranges.

Flat. All three males occupied distinct and exclusive ranges that they appeared to actively defend (hence they could properly be regarded as territories). They all showed evidence of involvement in past fights and on one memorable occasion I even witnessed two of them fighting. But usually I only saw the aftermath – several square metres of disturbance in the ground litter, usually with a wrecked radio-collar lying in the midst of it. It proved very difficult to keep radio-collars on male tree-kangaroos for any length of time.

'Simon', the one-eared animal I referred to earlier, had a small home range crammed in between the larger ranges of the other two males. He seemed to be only just hanging in there as both of his neighbours were bigger than him and in better condition. He appeared to suffer constant harassment and occasionally was found several hundred metres outside his range, in a dry creek bed off the south-west corner of the study area. Presumably it was a refuge to which he retreated when set upon by the other males.

Late in the study we captured a male that was in an even more desperate state than 'Simon'. We found this animal some distance from the main study area, living in sparse gallery forest abutting the dry bed of a small creek. Judging from the amount of wear on his teeth, he was a very old animal. With both of his ears shredded and a large pink scar at the base of his left ear, he looked like an old prize fighter. As well, he had a hole torn right through his lower left eyelid. The nails on his hind feet were almost completely worn away and this, as well as copious quantities of dry faecal pellets scattered about the creek bed, indicated that he lived in a very small range and spent a lot of his time moving along the creek bed on the abrasive rocks there. His only food seemed to be foliage from the Umbrella Tree (*Schefflera actinophylla*) that was abundant thereabouts and showed signs of heavy browsing. His fate seemed to be what was in store for old male tree-kangaroos, once they are unable to hold ground against their younger rivals in the rainforest.

Graeme Newell found that male Lumholtz's Tree-kangaroos also maintained discrete home ranges within their patch of forest. His radio-tracking data suggested that the males 'regularly came into contact with each other, often under antagonistic circumstances'. So it appears that they were also defending space and that the males of both species of Australian tree-kangaroo display territorial behaviour.

Use of space by New Guinea Tree-kangaroos

Apart from Will Betz's indirect estimate, based on dung pellet counts, of Matschie's Tree-kangaroos using between 0.7 and 1.6 hectares of forest, the only information we have on spatial requirements for New Guinea Tree-kangaroos is from a single radio-tracking study conducted by Liam Sterling and his colleagues on an Oxford University expedition there in 1991. They estimated a home range size of around 25 hectares for a single Matschie's Tree-kangaroo of unknown sex.

Keyt Fischer had a radio-collar on a subspecies of Doria's Tree-kangaroo (*D. dorianus notatus*) in the Mount Stolle region of Sandaun Province for a short time but, as far as I can ascertain, she did not report a home range size. Tim Flannery and Viare Kula also had radio-collars on several Scott's Tree-kangaroos (*D. scottae*) in the Torricelli Mountains, but unfortunately did not get enough positional fixes to make an estimate of the size of their range. One interesting fact to emerge from their study was that, in contrast to the primarily nocturnal activity pattern of the Australian tree-kangaroos studied, *D. scottae* seemed to be mainly active during the day.

This meagre amount of information is all we currently know about the spatial requirements of New Guinea tree-kangaroos.

9
Sex and reproduction

Broadly speaking, tree-kangaroos reproduction follows much the same pattern as other macropods. Gestation is brief with the new born (known as a neonate) emerging in a nearly embryonic condition. Appearances are deceptive, however, and the respiratory, olfactory, digestive and urinary systems of this queer little creature all appear to be functioning. As well, it is equipped with strongly developed forearms, clawed forepaws and, most important of all, with the inherent will to climb. As soon as it emerges from the cloacal opening, it has to climb – up the mother's belly fur and into her pouch. And it has to do it quickly or it won't survive. Once inside the pouch, it has to locate a suitable nipple (probably using its olfactory sense), attach to it and commence suckling. It's a big journey, particularly when you are only 45 days old.

Preceding this minor miracle of marsupial birth, many other things have to happen. There is a courtship between a male and female tree-kangaroo, a fruitful mating and a period of embryonic development (gestation) within the mother's uterus. Following birth there is a lengthy period of growth and development within the pouch. At the end of pouch life the young tree-kangaroo has to face what really amounts to a second birth – its exit from the pouch and entry into the dangerous world of the rainforest canopy. This marks the beginning of another lengthy phase of growth and learning that culminates in the young animal taking its place as an independent member of tree-kangaroo society.

Male reproductive behaviour

The only field observations of mating behaviour in wild tree-kangaroos that I know of are from my own studies of Bennett's Tree-kangaroo at Shipton's Flat. In the previous chapter I described how both the females and males of this species occupied discrete areas of forest; that is, they did not share their range with other adults of the same sex. But the ranges of the males and females did overlap and, as the male ranges are usually much larger than those of the females, a single male range usually encompasses several female ranges. The home range of my key adult male 'Dave', for example, included the ranges of three adult females.

It is informative to look at how 'Dave' moved around his range and interacted with the females. During the daylight hours 'Dave's' behaviour was similar to the females, spending most of his time sitting high up in the canopy in roost trees. At night, however, his behaviour was markedly different and his focus wasn't so much on trees with food in them as it was on trees with females in them. He spent many a balmy September night sharing a tree with one of the resident females. Sometimes he spent several nights in a row with the same female. In one memorable 48-hour period, he was seen in the company of all three resident females in succession. He didn't have the field to himself, however, as a large male from an adjoining territory ('Tom') was seen with some of the same females on the nights when 'Dave' wasn't around.

So what was going on? In the preceding chapter I described how male Bennett's Tree-kangaroos vigorously exclude other males from their patch of forest and it isn't just real estate that is being defended (see figure below). Bennett's Tree-kangaroo proved to be a seasonal breeder and two months after

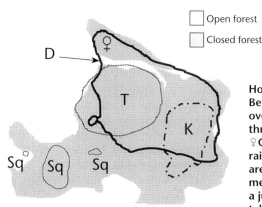

Open forest

Closed forest

Home range of the adult male Bennett's Tree-kangaroo 'Dave' overlapping the home ranges of the three females ('Tricia', 'Kiwi' and ♀G) that lived in the same patch of rainforest. Home range boundaries are the 95% isopleth of the harmonic mean centre of activity. Sq = 'Squeely' a juvenile tree-kangaroo that was taken by a python (see page 85).

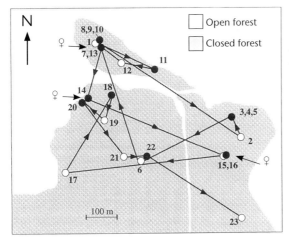

The track of the male Bennett's Tree-kangaroo 'Dave' between his diurnal roost trees (o) and other trees that he visited at night (●) during early September 1990. The nocturnal fixes marked with the ♀ symbol indicate locations when he was together with a female in the same tree. The numbers indicate the sequence of the fixes, and the lines and arrowheads respectively indicate the shortest distance and general direction of travel between them.

these observations were made two of the females that 'Dave' had been seen with had small young in their pouch. Late September, it seems, is the peak of the breeding season. In early September 'Dave' was probably hanging out with the females to keep other males away and make sure that he was the first to mate with them when they came into oestrous. This sort of male behaviour, known as 'mate guarding', is common in many mammal groups, including macropods.

Information from captive breeding studies
As I have already said several times, wild tree-kangaroos are both difficult to observe and capture. As a consequence the specifics of their reproductive biology are poorly known. What detailed knowledge we have comes from captive studies and I relied heavily on these to interpret the behaviours that I just described.

Lumholtz's Tree-kangaroo
The most extensive captive study of an Australian species has been on Lumholtz's Tree-kangaroo. Peter Johnson, from the Queensland National Parks and Wildlife Service, has maintained a colony of this species at Townsville, in Far North Queensland, for many years. Among his many valuable observations, he has provided a detailed account of their mating behaviour.

When a female Lumholtz's Tree-kangaroo is in oestrus the male spends a lot of time near her, frequently sniffing around her cloaca and pouch area. The male continues this behaviour for some time, probably until he is convinced she is in oestrus and likely to be receptive to mating. He then moves behind her and proceeds to rub his head, neck and shoulders on her cloaca while the female supports her weight with her forepaws on the ground. The result of this is that the neck and shoulders of the male become 'covered in exudates from the cloaca'. So, adorned in his odoriferous raiment, the male proceeds to the mating, clasping the female from behind with his forelimbs around her thorax in the typical macropod fashion, she with her 'hindquarters raised and forepaws on the ground'. All the time the female is making 'a soft trumpeting sound' with her head and neck trembling. Mating lasts between 10 and 35 minutes and the performance is sometimes repeated three times a day for up to three days. Usually this takes place on the ground but an elevated feeding platform in their enclosure was occasionally used. A copulatory plug, to inhibit the semen from other males from entering the tract, is evident after most matings.

So this is part of what 'Dave' was doing in the month of September. He was also busy guarding three females spread over 20 hectares of rainforest, at the same time fighting off other males who were as interested in mating with these females as he was.

Female reproduction

Another advantage of doing reproductive research on captive animals is that it permits continuous monitoring of females and enables very accurate measurements of both the oestrous cycle (the length of time between successive ovulations) and the period of gestation (the time that elapses between mating and giving birth) to be made.

Relying only on observations of their behaviour, Peter Johnson estimated that the oestrous cycles in female Lumholtz's varies between 47 and 64 days with a mean of 56.4 days. He further estimated the length of gestation to be between 42 and 48 days with a mean of 44.8 days. This is an extremely long gestation period compared with other macropods.

Townsville, where this captive colony was held, is just outside the natural range of Lumholtz's Tree-kangaroo and, as the animals were kept in outside cages, they would have experienced much the same seasonal conditions as their free-living relatives. Hence the fact that these animals showed no seasonal pattern in their reproductive activities (i.e. they mated and bore young throughout the year) suggests that they may do likewise in the wild. If this is the case then Lumholtz's differs markedly from Bennett's Tree-kangaroo, which shows a strong seasonal pattern of reproductive activity. Of the 11 pouch young I saw in my study population, 10 were born in the wet season – eight in the early wet (November to January) and two in the late wet (February to April). However, my study population was living in monsoon forest and their breeding activity could be an adaptation to the marked seasonality of this forest. Lumholtz's Tree-kangaroos mainly inhabit the upland forests of the

Atherton Tablelands and don't experience the seasonal extremes of the drier forests further north.

Postpartum oestrus and embryonic diapause

Peter Johnson made other important observations of female reproduction in his captive Lumholtz's Tree-kangaroos. For one, he noted that unlike many macropod species the females did not show a postpartum oestrus. Postpartum oestrus is when a female comes into oestrus and mates a very short time after she has given birth. As a consequence the female is simultaneously pregnant, with a tiny embryo developing in her uterus, and carrying a small young in her pouch.

Another reproductive adaptation, known as embryonic diapause, occurs together with postpartum oestrus in many macropods. With this the embryo goes into a state of quiescence at a very early stage of its development (when it comprises about 100 cells and is known as a blastocyst) and remains in this state of suspended animation in the uterus for some time. Development is usually re-initiated when the older sibling in the pouch is weaned.

Whether or not embryonic diapause occurs in tree-kangaroos is still a moot question. Back in the late 1960s, when he was managing a large collection of tree-kangaroos at the Baiyer River Sanctuary in the Western Highlands of Papua and New Guinea, Graeme George thought he had evidence that it did occur. At that time breeding colonies of mostly wild-caught animals were being used to propagate some species and, as part of this programme, the pouches of all females were checked monthly. A female *Dendrolagus goodfellowi* was brought in from the wild with a small young in her pouch and kept apart from the other animals until she had weaned this young. She duly did so but, during a regular pouch check a couple of months later, she was found to have a tiny neonate in her pouch. Graeme George was confident that she had been kept separated from mature males all the time she had been in captivity and duly reported the incident as evidence that 'delayed implantation of the blastocyst occurs in *Dendrolagus*'.

Peter Johnson found no evidence of embryonic diapause in his work on *D. lumholtzi*. Neither did Heath and his colleagues in their exhaustive studies of reproduction in *D. matschiei* at the National Zoological Park in Washington DC. It may occur but the evidence is contradictory and, on balance, it is doubtful that it does. Maybe, all those years ago at Baiyer River, a male Goodfellow's did find his way into the same cage as that female. As biologists who have worked in New Guinea all know, it's not called 'The Land of the Unexpected' for nothing.

Peter Johnson found that the female Lumholtz's in his care usually came into oestrus two months or so after their young had permanently left the pouch. The young were just over 11 months old at the time (nine months at permanent pouch emergence) and they continued to suckle their mother for another month or two after this. (By this time the teat was so elongated that it protruded from the pouch opening.) One consequence of this is a very long interval between births – it averaged 1.4 years for these females, which means Lumholtz's Tree-kangaroo has relatively low fecundity compared with other macropods.

Peter Johnson was also able to make some interesting observations of the progress of young Lumholtz's Tree-kangaroos once they leave the pouch. Their exploration of the outside world begins when they are between six and seven months old and only just furred. After such a long period of solitary confinement they appear exceptionally eager to get on with life and begin with a series of short excursions, usually climbing around on the wire netting surrounding their enclosure.

They are precocious in their climbing ability but sadly deficient in hopping skills and their mothers appear to be concerned about this ineptness. Peter Johnson observed one female standing behind her young, gripping its tail with both her paws to stop it getting away and, despite its loud squeals of protest, encouraging it to get back into her pouch. In view of the great appetite of Amethystine Pythons for young Bennett's Tree-kangaroos (see Chapter 6) mother tree-kangaroos are wise to restrain such exuberance.

After a brief period of frenetic activity (lasting only a week or two) the young quieted down for the next couple of months until they permanently exited the pouch. In summing up the interactions between mother and young that took place over this period Peter Johnson sagely observed that 'female *D. lumholtzi* invest significantly in the education of their young to cope with their complex and predominantly arboreal lifestyle' and speculated whether this might have something to do with the long birth interval.

Matschie's Tree-kangaroo

Matschie's Tree-kangaroo (*D. matschiei*) also breeds well in captivity and there are colonies held at a number of zoos in the United States of America. A great deal of research has been done on animals from these colonies, particularly those at the National Zoological Park in Washington DC and at the Woodland Park Zoo in Seattle, and the details of their reproductive biology are well known.

Lisa Dabek, formerly at Woodland Park but now at the Roger Williams Park Zoo on Rhode Island, measured the length of the oestrus cycle using a more precise method than the behavioural observations relied on by Peter Johnson. Her technique, known as faecal steroid analysis, involved measuring the daily concentrations of the reproductive hormones, oestrogen and progestin, in the faecal pellets of females. From her results she estimated the oestrus cycle of a female Matschie's to be between 54.2 (based on the interval between peak concentrations of progestin in the faeces) and 56.8 days (based on oestrogen peaks). These figures are very close to the 56.4 days estimate for Lumholtz's Tree-kangaroo.

In the colony held at the National Zoological Park in Washington DC, adult females produce their first young when they are 2–2.5 years of age and are capable of producing young at 12-month intervals after this. No copulations have been observed immediately postpartum and, as stated earlier, no evidence of embryonic diapause has been found. Births occur in all months of the year, with an average gestation period of 44 days. Young first venture out of the pouch when they are seven months old and permanently emerge at 10 months of age. One notable female continued breeding until she was 14 years old and longevity of 20 years has been reported for captive *D. matschiei*.

Key features of tree-kangaroo reproductive biology

The most striking thing about the reproductive parameters of *D. lumholtzi* and *D. matschiei* is the high degree of similarity. This is a little surprising because Lumholtz's is supposedly a member of the 'primitive' grade of tree-kangaroos and lives in the relatively dry rainforests of north-eastern Queensland, whereas Matschie's comes from the continually wet upland rainforests of New Guinea and is considered to be further along the tree-kangaroo evolutionary path than its Australian cousin. Yet both are continuous breeders with oestrus cycles of 54–56 days in length, both gestate their young for the same extremely long period of 44 days and neither show any evidence of a postpartum oestrus or delayed implantation of the blastocyst.

Some of these parameters are of intrinsic biological interest only, whereas others probably reflect adaptations that these formerly terrestrial macropods have made to survive in their adopted, rainforest home.

Timing of breeding

The captive studies suggest that tree-kangaroos breed continuously but this didn't seem to be the case with the free-living *D. bennettianus* that I studied. I have already suggested that captive studies may not be absolutely reliable on this point. Captivity ameliorates the harsh realities of living in the wild. Food is always available and captive animals seldom experience seasonal shortages of any essential resources. Continuous breeding is not surprising in *D. matschiei* because they normally live in the higher altitude equatorial rainforests of New Guinea – a largely aseasonal environment where there is little change in resources from one month to the next. However, the same is not true for some of the habitats of Australian tree-kangaroos. My field data suggested that Bennett's Tree-kangaroo bred seasonally and, if we look at the habitat it lives in, it's not hard to understand why.

Seasonality is pronounced in the lowlands around Shipton's Flat. Very little rain falls between July and October and the early summer is extremely hot. This is reflected in the closed forests of the area which are mainly semi-deciduous monsoonal vine forests. A seasonal pattern in breeding in the local tree-kangaroos is therefore not surprising. Most herbivores living in the area appear to synchronise their breeding with the beginning of the wet. Even the 'domestic cattle', which live a substantially feral lifestyle, are seasonal breeders with most giving birth to their calves at the beginning of the wet season.

It is not difficult to attribute an adaptive advantage to tree-kangaroos that produce their young at this time. By doing so the heaviest lactational load on the female, which occurs during the last three months of pouch life, would occur during April/May – one of the most reliably wet periods of the year. Moisture availability could be a significant constraint later in the year. Tree-kangaroos have to rely on dietary intake for water during the dry season (September until March/April) and a lactating female could experience moisture stress. As well, young born at the beginning of one wet season will be fully weaned by the beginning of the next, in synchrony with the abundance of nutritious new leaves and fruit that occurs then.

Postpartum oestrus, embryonic diapause and fecundity

Postpartum oestrus with embryonic diapause is almost universal among the rock-wallabies (*Petrogale* spp.), which are the most closely related macropod genus to *Dendrolagus*. Although Graeme George produced some evidence for its occurrence in *D. goodfellowi*, diapause hasn't been conclusively observed in captive studies of either *D. matschiei* or *D. lumholtzi*. Exhaustive field studies of wild populations are needed to resolve this issue, and as such studies would need to be invasive, it is unlikely they ever will be done.

What is the significance of these unusual reproductive adaptations and what advantages do they confer on the macropods that possess them?

Essentially postpartum oestrus and embryonic diapause achieve two things: acting together they shorten the interval between births and therefore increase the lifetime fecundity of a female. Acting alone, embryonic diapause confers an advantage on kangaroo species that frequently experience droughts and the concomitant critical shortages of food and water. Female kangaroos often enter anoestrus at this time; that is, they stop ovulating and abandon their pouch young to ensure their own survival. Even in such a debilitated state, they'll often still have a tiny blastocyst in their uterus. Energetically it costs them nothing to maintain and, as soon as the drought breaks and nutritious shoots of fresh grass appear, its development is reactivated and the female gives birth within the month. They don't need a male around to produce this new individual and it is a truly wonderful adaptation for a creature that is occasionally driven into desperately low numbers in the harsh deserts of inland Australia.

Tree-kangaroos usually don't experience such privations. They live in the forested coastal mountains and, although droughts are not unheard of here, they don't occur very frequently. And, as I argued in Chapter 5, one of the possible reasons tree-kangaroos abandoned the terrestrial lifestyle in the first place was to get at the more reliably available food supply of the canopy.

Returning to the reduction in birth interval and enhanced lifetime fecundity that a postpartum oestrus would confer, the question is whether this is something that would be advantageous to tree-kangaroos? Well, maybe, but it depends on the overall 'reproductive strategy' of the species.

Population biologists talk of two overall reproductive strategies that animal populations adopt – they are either 'r' strategists or 'K' strategists. Without getting involved in the detail, what this essentially means is that a female either opts for quantity or quality in the production of young: 'r' strategists produce lots of young but don't invest much time in ensuring that they all survive. Enough do for the species to survive. K strategists on the other hand don't have many offspring but they spend a lot of time nurturing them to ensure a high survival rate. For a variety of reasons, most of which I have already mentioned, the tree-kangaroo lifestyle commits them to being K strategists. They live in a complex and dangerous world and if any of their young are to survive they need to spend a lot of time educating them about their environment. A reduced birth interval and a higher fecundity rate would not confer any advantage.

The net effect of all this is that tree-kangaroos have a relatively low rate of reproduction. The full significance of this will become apparent when we get to the final chapter on their conservation.

Length of gestation

The gestation length in *Dendrolagus* of 44 days is the longest recorded for any marsupial. It exceeds by six days that of the next longest gestator, the Grey Kangaroo (*Macropus giganteus*), which, as its scientific name suggests, is a big animal. Males over 70 kg are regularly recorded and this makes them more than five times the size of the biggest of the tree-kangaroos. Body size appears to have nothing to do with it, so why then is gestation so long in *Dendrolagus* spp? A good question and no one has yet come up with a satisfactory answer.

Maternal care

In his captive studies Peter Johnson commented that female Lumholtz's appear to invest a significant amount of time in educating their young and that this may be necessary for them to cope with their complex environment. The length of time that the young remain in close association with their mothers was also something that impressed me about the free-living Bennett's tree-kangaroos. Usually the bond between them persisted well beyond weaning, with some remaining in close contact with their mothers until they were more than two years old. Liz Proctor-Grey noted similar behaviour in wild Lumholtz's Tree-kangaroos. One young she was monitoring was still following its mother around when it was 19 months old, and another male was still residing in his mother's territory, although not closely following her around, when he was 22 months old.

There would be many advantages for a young tree-kangaroo in doing this. In the case of Bennett's Tree-kangaroo, for example, its chances of surviving Amethystine Pythons would be greatly enhanced. Primarily, however, it gives the young time to gain experience of the wide variety of food resources that they can eat and, more importantly, of the plants that they should avoid. Staple foods, such as leaves from palatable species, are always available, but other foods can be sparsely distributed and only available for a short time during the year. Some, particularly fruits, vary greatly in their abundance between years. The green fruit of one of the native olives (*Chionanthus ramiflorus*), for example, was available for a month or so in the first year of my study and was a very popular food but, because of unseasonal rain at the time of flowering, little fruit was produced the following year. Some seasonally available resources are thinly scattered over a wide area and only available for a very short time. The petioles of the newly emerging leaves of the Leichardt Tree (*Nauclea orientalis*) would fall into this category. They are highly favoured by tree-kangaroos but the trees are very sparsely distributed and the emergence of new leaves only occurs for a very short time late in the dry season. These examples all suggest that the ability of young tree-kangaroos to exploit transient food resources and deal with sophisticated predators would be enhanced by the knowledge and experience they gain while accompanying their mothers.

The brain of a tree-kangaroo

My interpretation of the extended period of maternal care by tree-kangaroos places some emphasis on their cognitive ability and leaf-eating marsupials are generally not considered to be particularly intelligent creatures. Initially, I inclined to this point of view because before studying Bennett's Tree-kangaroo, I had worked with koalas for many years. Koalas have very stereotyped

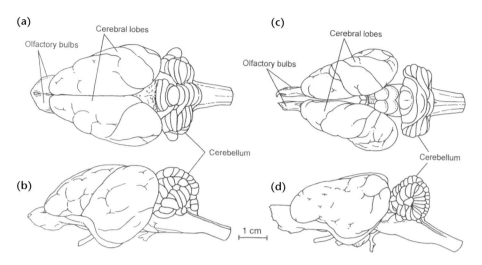

Scale drawings of the brain of a Lumholtz's Tree-kangaroo (*Dendrolagus lumholtzi*) (a, b) and a Koala (*Phascolarctos cinereus*) (c, d).

behaviour and certainly gave the impression that they are not very intelligent. Cute, yes, but not smart.

The Koala and Lumholtz's Tree-kangaroo have similar body weights but, looking at the relative sizes of their brains, it is seems that the brain of a Lumholtz's Tree-kangaroo is significantly larger than that of a Koala. Superficially, this would suggest that the Tree-kangaroo is 'brighter' than the Koala, but a more objective measure of the relative intelligence of each species is needed to make a convincing argument.

Developing such a measure has always been problematic for biologists. Raymond Dart, an early primatologist, was one of the first to grapple with it and developed an index of the ratio of brain weight to body weight for hominids. In recent years a similar index, called an encephalisation index or EI, has been developed for marsupials by three neuro-anatomists – John Nelson, from Monash University, Australia, Heinz Stephan, from the Max Planck Institute for Brain Research, Germany, and George Baron, from the University of Montreal, Canada. To determine an EI for a species they first postulate a brain weight to body weight ratio for what they nominate as the basal mammal. They selected the eutherian shrew *Sorex* sp. as their basal mammal. Therefore, an animal's EI is the ratio of its brain weight to the brain weight projected for a basal mammal of the same body weight multiplied by 100.

Their results indicate that, for their body size, tree-kangaroos have one of the larger brains to be found among marsupials. The four species they measured have a mean EI of 244. For *D. bennettianus* the figure is 246 and for

D. goodfellowi 277, which compares with an EI of 125 for the Koala and a mean of 193 for the 14 other macropod species that they measured.

So it does seem that, compared with most marsupials, tree-kangaroos are relatively 'bright'. John Nelson and his colleagues don't claim that the EI is an exact measure of relative intelligence but they do believe that species with a relatively high index have greater potential for integrating complex sensory information.

10
Conservation

Ihave left the subject of tree-kangaroo conservation until this last chapter, but this isn't intended to suggest that it is less important than the other topics discussed. On the contrary, it is probably the most important. In New Guinea, the heartland of tree-kangaroo diversity, there have been numerous local extinctions during the past century. Many populations of the once widespread Doria's (*Dendrolagus dorianus*) and Goodfellow's (*D. goodfellowi*) Tree-kangaroos have disappeared and many others are on the verge of extinction. Perhaps more disturbing is the fact that we know so little about the majority of the tree-kangaroos species inhabiting the island of New Guinea that we can only guess at the current conservation status of most of them.

The situation isn't perfect for the two Australian species (*D. lumholtzi* and *D. bennettianus*) either, but it is better than for most of their New Guinea cousins. Here I will give the specific information, beginning with their conservation status.

Current conservation status of tree-kangaroos

The International Union for the Conservation of Nature attempts to estimate the conservation status of each wild species. As you would expect, it is a very difficult undertaking because many of the planet's rarer species come from remote regions (such as New Guinea) and their biology is usually poorly known. Despite the difficulties the Union tries to be objective, seeking the views of biologists most familiar with the species and relying on a set of carefully thought out criteria in making the assessments.

A Red List of Threatened Species, which categorises species according to their endangered status, is regularly published by the Union. The categories range from a relatively benign 'near threatened' through to the precarious 'critically endangered'. The most recent review of the status of tree-kangaroos, based on the recommendations of the Australasian Marsupial and Monotreme Specialist Group, appeared in 1994 and is reproduced in Table 10.1.

Table 10.1 Conservation status of tree-kangaroos according to Tim Flannery (1996) and the International Union for the Conservation of Nature Red List of Threatened Species (IUCN 2003)

Scientific name	Common name	Red List	Flannery
Australian spp.			
D. bennettianus	Bennett's Tree-kangaroo	Low risk	Secure
D. lumholtzi	Lumholtz's Tree-kangaroo	Low risk	Secure
New Guinea spp.			
D. inustus	Grizzled Tree-kangaroo	DD	–
D. i. inustus	Grizzled Tree-kangaroo	–	DD
D. i. finschi	Finsch's Tree-kangaroo	–	VU
D. dorianus	Doria's Tree-kangaroo	VU	–
D. d. dorianus	Doria's Tree-kangaroo	–	DD
D. d. notatus	Ifola	–	EN
D. d. stellarum	Seri's Tree-kangaroo	–	VU
D. d. mayri	Wondiwoi Tree-kangaroo	–	DD
D. scottae	Scott's Tree-kangaroo	EN	CR
D. scottae subsp. indet.	Fiwo	–	VU
D. goodfellowi	Goodfellow's Tree-kangaroo	EN	–
D. g. goodfellowi	Goodfellow's Tree-kangaroo	–	DD
D. g. buergersi	Timboyok	–	EN
D. g. pulcherrimus	Golden-mantled Tree-kangaroo	–	CR
D. matschiei	Huon Tree-kangaroo	EN	EN
D. mbaiso	Dingiso	VU	VU
D. spadix	Lowland Tree-kangaroo	DD	DD
D. ursinus	Vogelkopt Tree-kangaroo	DD	VU

DD, data deficient; VU, vulnerable; EN, endangered; CR, critically endangered.

Tim Flannery spent nearly a decade collecting mammals in New Guinea and his is the most informed view of the current status of the tree-kangaroos there. His rankings, which first appeared in 1996, are more comprehensive than those of the International Union for the Conservation of Nature because he includes all of the subspecies of tree-kangaroos from both Papua New Guinea and West Papua.

With the exception of the two Australian species, it is a very disturbing picture: of the 15 species and subspecies of tree-kangaroo described from the island of New Guinea, two are critically endangered, three are endangered and five are vulnerable. For the remaining five taxa there just is not enough information.

Conservation of the Australian species

Lumholtz's Tree-kangaroo

At the present time the conservation status of both of the Australian species is relatively good. The more studied of these species, Lumholtz's Tree-kangaroo, now has its main populations on the Atherton Tablelands where there is intensive agriculture and a large human population. Many of its conservation problems can be attributed to these two factors.

In the late 1990s, after completing several years of research on Lumholtz's Tree-kangaroo, Graeme Newell identified what he saw as the issues with their conservation and discussed the measures he thought might be useful in addressing them. He listed these issues as loss of habitat, road deaths, predation by dogs, and disease.

Loss of habitat

When it comes to looking at the conservation needs of Australia's tree-kangaroos, the one salient fact that cannot be ignored is that their primary habitat, tropical rainforest, is very rare. It covers less than 0.2% of the land area of Australia. Populations of *D. lumholtzi* are still found in about 5500 square kilometres of this forest, which is not an insignificant area, but, as I've already discussed, they are not evenly distributed through it. They are far more abundant in some forest types than others. Their favourite appears to be the vine forests that grow on the highly fertile, volcanic soils. Unfortunately for them, these areas are also highly valued for their agricultural potential and, in the 200 years since Europeans first arrived in north Queensland, most of this forest has been cleared and replaced with crops or pasture. There is now less than 20 square kilometres of this forest left. Some lies within the Wet Tropics World Heritage Area and is secure, but most of it is privately owned and still at risk. In fact, the main stimulus for Graeme Newell to consider the conservation prognosis for Lumholtz's Tree-kangaroo was the partial clearing of his study site by the owner of the land.

Newell canvassed a range of measures that might be used to conserve these privately owned forest remnants. He thought financial incentives to the landowners were the most likely to succeed and put the argument that if the Australian Government was prepared to offer tax rebates for the conservation of privately owned heritage buildings, then why couldn't the same offer be made to conserve these 'heritage' forests. Why not indeed? Another approach he suggested was to raise public awareness via education. The general public in Australia know a lot about koalas, but are ignorant of some of the more amazing creatures – kangaroos that climb trees for example. If the animals' rarity and beauty were more widely appreciated then these private landowners might place more value on the tree-kangaroos.

Predation

Since they have been sharing the same forest for between 3000 and 5000 years, dingoes can rightly be regarded as a 'natural' predator of tree-kangaroos. However, the delicate equilibrium that once existed between them was upset by the arrival of European settlers and their soul mates, domesticated dogs. Many of these have become feral, interbred with and boosted the fecundity of the wild dog populations (dingoes only have one litter a year whereas domestic dogs can have two). Many other nominally domestic dogs live a substantially feral existence, roaming free at night and preying on wildlife. The net result is that tree-kangaroos now have more canine predators than ever before to contend with. And because of European settlers' widescale clearing of forest, tree-kangaroos often have to cross wide stretches of open country when moving between forest patches and, in such an exposed situation, they are easy meat for dogs.

This is not a simple problem to address. Public education programmes to encourage people to lock their dogs up at night is one approach and it is something that municipal councils occasionally undertake. Eradicating feral dogs is more difficult – it usually involves trapping or laying poison baits and few people support this.

Planting corridors of native trees to link remnant patches of forest and give tree-kangaroos sanctuary in their journeys across open country is another solution and a much effort has gone into such plantings by voluntary groups, especially on the Atherton Tablelands. However, farmers are understandably reluctant to sacrifice productive land and so most of these plantings have been on unproductive country, steep creek banks and the like.

A novel method to ensure safe passage for tree-kangaroos across prime pastureland while leaving the pasture intact is being trialled by John Kanowski, from Griffith University in Queensland, and Nigel Tucker from Queensland Parks and Wildlife Service. They have erected a series of poles, safe-havens with an access rope and a cross-bar to sit on, at 40 metre intervals across an open area of pasture lying between two rainforest blocks. A neat idea, the efficacy of which is yet to be evaluated.

Roadkill

The rainforests of the Atherton Tablelands are also traversed by a network of sealed roads and many tree-kangaroos are killed by cars. Subadult males suffer the greatest mortality, probably because they are the most mobile group, particularly during the breeding season when they move about a lot to avoid conflict with adult males. In a polygamous species such as the tree-kangaroos, a high mortality rate in subadult males doesn't threaten the viability of the population, but it is very distressing for such beautiful animals to be unnecessarily killed. Once again there are no simple measures to deal with the problem. Public education and road signs warning of tree-kangaroos and encouraging motorists to slow down seem to be the only answers.

Bennett's Tree-kangaroo

Bennett's Tree-kangaroo has a more restricted geographic range than Lumholtz's, occupying a total area probably less than 2500 square kilometres. This is not a very large geographical range for a species, but almost all of it is north of the Daintree River and within the Wet Tropics World Heritage Area so most of it is protected by United Nations Charter. Clearing of the forest is not allowed so it is a very secure tree-kangaroo habitat.

The human population density within this area is also much lower than it is within the range of Lumholtz's Tree-kangaroo, so there aren't the same concerns about excessive numbers of tree-kangaroos being killed by either motor cars or domestic dogs. However, pig hunting is a popular recreation and the hunting dogs are a threat to tree-kangaroos, particularly at the southern end of Bennett's range where most people live.

As I discussed earlier, there is evidence of direct hunting having a substantial impact on Bennett's Tree-kangaroo in pre-European times, particularly the abundance of the lowland populations. These hunters were mainly indigenous Gugu Yalangi men but their reliance on traditional foods has declined markedly over the past 50 years. Unless this changes, and hunting becomes popular again, it poses no threat to Bennett's Tree-kangaroo. But, as we will see in the next section, this is not the case in New Guinea.

Conservation of the New Guinea species

Over-hunting

As I pointed out in the previous chapter, tree-kangaroos have a very low rate of reproduction. One consequence of this is that their populations are very susceptible to overkill; that is, when deaths due to hunting outnumber births. At the present time many tree-kangaroo populations in New Guinea are in this situation and it is a very serious threat to their survival.

Graeme George was one of the first to draw attention to this. In the early 1970s, while Superintendent of the Baiyer River Sanctuary he went on a field trip to the Wahgi Valley and, as is normal on such trips, he employed some local landowners to assist him. Two of these men, Konga and Raia, were particularly valuable assistants as they were locally renowned for both their hunting prowess and knowledge of wildlife. Graeme George already had concerns about the current status of tree-kangaroos in the Highlands and, in campfire conversations during the trip, he was dismayed to have his worst fears confirmed by these two hunters. Mogolip (Doria's Tree-kangaroo, *D. dorianus*) was a prime game species that Konga and Raia had hunted for years but now they were lamenting that 'each time they went hunting, they had to venture higher and higher into the mountains to find any mogolip – acknowledging that their activities over the years had eliminated their quarry in more accessible forests on the lower mountain slopes'.

Tim Flannery relates similar stories told to him by old men in the Torricelli Mountains when he was collecting there in the early 1990s. Although Grizzled Tree-kangaroos are still regularly caught, one of the other tree-kangaroo species in this area, known as tenkile (Scott's Tree-kangaroo, *D. scottae*), is now rarely seen and thought to be critically endangered. Yet '[The] oldest hunters (60–70 years old) remember a time in their youth when tenkile were common'.

More recently, Will Betz and Lisa Dabek have conducted extensive interviews with landowners on the Huon Peninsula and the overriding impression

Photo: R. Martin

Hunters in the Torricelli Mountains returning to camp after a morning hunting tree-kangaroos.

The catch is three Finsch's Tree-kangaroos, *Dendrolagus inustus finschi*.

they had was the perceived status of Matschie's, the local tree-kangaroo species, had deteriorated in recent times. Taken together, these accounts suggest the phenomenon of species decline is widespread in New Guinea.

The pouch young of females killed by hunters are often kept alive and taken back to the village to be hand-raised.

The main reason for this decline appears to be hunting. This is partly related to an increase in the efficiency of the hunters – steel axes and bush knives enable them to quickly cut tracks through the forest and even cut down a tree with a tree-kangaroos in it, modern firearms enable them to shoot tree-kangaroos out of the canopy – but largely it is because there are now a lot more hunters. Tim Flannery points out that the human population of the Torricelli Mountains has probably increased three-fold during the lifetimes of the old hunters he interviewed. Graeme George attributes this population increase to increased longevity and a rise in the birth rate, which he links to the general improvement in the health, social and economic conditions of indigenous New Guineans during the past century.

The hunters also have access to more of the forest. Many new roads have been built in New Guinea and new villages have sprung up along these roads, bringing hunters within easy walking distance of the previously inaccessible forest. Also, in pre-European times some forest areas weren't visited by hunters because they were believed to be inhabited by powerful spirits (ples masolai) and the hunters were fearful of going there. These 'ples masolai' were de facto conservation zones for tree-kangaroos, but such traditional beliefs are less widely held now.

Other areas that weren't visited by hunters were the tracts of forest between the territories of warring tribes. Tribal warfare was almost continuous in some parts of New Guinea in pre-European times and these 'no-man's lands' would have represented a considerable area of refuge for tree-kangaroos.

So what can be done to reduce the impact of hunting?

Before I attempt to answer that question let me say a few words about the role hunting plays in New Guinea village life. It's usually only the men who go hunting and their reason for doing so is more cultural/recreational than subsistence. As Graeme George put it, 'when local hunters kill animals in the mountains they cook and eat them on the spot'. The only time tree-kangaroo meat finds its way back to the village is when it is required for a ceremonial feast. So it is fair to say that tree-kangaroo meat doesn't make a significant contribution to the protein intake of the women and children of the village.

A second important point to understand is the role of the hunting dogs. Carl Lumholtz was probably the first European to recognise what indigenous hunters from Australia and New Guinea have known for eons; that it is virtually impossible to find tree-kangaroos in thick rainforest without the assistance of a dog. And just any dog won't do. Good tree-kangaroo dogs are rare and special creatures.

When they were working among the Karam people of the Schrader Mountains, the late Ralph Bulmer and Jim Menzies (from the University of

Photo: R. Martin

'Sime', the most efficient tree-kangaroo killer I have ever seen, with a garland, or 'bilas', conferred on him to mark a successful hunt.

Papua New Guinea) recognised that most of their hunting dogs were domesticated New Guinea wild dogs (*Canis familiaris hallstromi*), also known as the New Guinea Singing Dog. The hunters used to rob the litters of wild dogs and raise the pups in the village. Once mature, they often developed into formidable hunting dogs.

The best tree-kangaroo dog I've seen, a black devil named 'Sime' from Wilbete Village in the Torricelli Mountains, probably had that sort of pedigree. For such a small dog, 'Sime' had huge canines and one of the defining characters of *Canis familiaris hallstromi* is a canine that is greater than 10% of the skull length.

However, as Will Betz has recognised, hunting dogs made of the 'right stuff' – that is, having that mixture of 'inborn aggression, intelligence and tenacity' that make them so good in the bush – generally aren't well suited for village life. They need plenty of work and unless they are hunted frequently, they get bored and cause strife, usually 'attacking other dogs or killing chickens' around the village. New Guineans value their livestock and an owner must pay compensation for whatever damage his dog does. Failing that, the dog will be killed. If the owner doesn't do it then someone will do it for him. This can sometimes happen on a grand scale. Ralph Bulmer and Jim Menzies reported that when poultry keeping was being developed by the Karam in the mid-1960s, almost all the dogs in the valley were killed off. This was evidently as good for the tree-kangaroos as it was for the chickens and by the early 1970s large game animals were 'more numerous that they'd been for years'.

This observation suggests a link between tree-kangaroos conservation and the wellbeing of the New Guinea people. Will Betz points out that in order to establish a conservation ethos in New Guinea there is a need to engage the local people by facilitating local economic and social development in their area. Encouraging villagers to keep livestock would not only increase the amount of protein in the diet of village women and children, it would also provide a substantial disincentive to the keeping of hunting dogs.

Australian Volunteers International is supporting Jim and Jean Thomas in a similar type of programme in the Torricelli Mountains of north-western New Guinea. Two of the three species of tree-kangaroos in this region, namely the tenkile (*D. scottae*) and the Golden-mantled Tree-kangaroo (*D. goodfellowi pulcherrimus*), are critically endangered because of hunting and the Thomases are trialling ways to discourage it.

One is to get villagers to agree to a hunting moratorium and so far some 14 villages in the area have agreed. The Thomases try to visit all the villages regularly, both to encourage people to keep observing the moratoria and to employ some of the villagers in surveys for tree-kangaroos in the surrounding mountains. Jean Thomas is also teaching about nutrition in the local schools and, as part of this, encouraging the locals to increase their protein intake by farming rabbits. The Thomases provide the material to build the hutches and, once that's done, supply a breeding pair of rabbits.

Will Betz describes a variant of this approach on the Huon Peninsula, where he has been studying Matschie's Tree-kangaroo. Rather than moratoria, he suggests a network of relatively small reserves that are fully protected from hunting or other resource extraction. These reserves are clan owned and managed (there are usually a number of closely related families or clans living in each village) and the intervening forest that linked the reserves would still be hunted. But for any of these programmes to succeed the New Guinea villagers will have to believe there is some value in setting aside part of the forest.

Belief systems

I've already mentioned how the declining influence of ancient beliefs has lead New Guineans to disregard taboos on hunting in some areas (the ples masolai). To compensate, Will Betz believes that some sort of conservation ethic needs to be integrated into the existing traditional or Christian belief systems.

There is already evidence of how potent an alteration to a belief system can be. In the Maimafu area (near the Crater Mountains in the Eastern Highlands) many villagers have converted to the Seventh Day Adventist (SDA) Church, which is the main missionary organisation in the area. The SDA Church has extensive dietary laws, including a prohibition on the consumption of 'unclean' meat. According to the Book of the Old Testament on which they rely, the only 'clean' meat comes from animals that have 'the hoof divided and cheweth the cud' (Leviticus 11.3). There aren't many animals that fit these criteria in the rainforests of New Guinea and the meat of all of the traditional game species is certainly 'unclean'. Will Betz believes that the adoption of SDA beliefs in this area is already having a positive impact on the local abundance of tree-kangaroos.

Loss of habitat

Will Betz considers deforestation and forest degradation as the second biggest threat facing New Guinea tree-kangaroos. Deforestation rates in New Guinea are not the highest in the Asia-Pacific but logging is very destructive and the industry continues to expand. For example, logging is not yet a conservation issue in the Huon, but there are proposals to log the montane forests in the some of the best areas of the range of Matschie's Tree-kangaroo, such as the uninhabited Cromwell Mountains.

Another looming threat is the impact of climate change on the montane forests. In the unprecedented dry weather of the most recent El Niño event (1997–98) huge areas of New Guinea's forests were burnt. More forest was destroyed and degraded in this 12-month period than has been lost in the previous 20 years. Climate change and global warming pose a significant threat to the habitat of tree-kangaroos living in the higher altitude forests.

Radical conservation options

What if the current programmes encouraging the local conservation of tree-kangaroos in New Guinea fail? They easily could because they mostly operate on shoestring budgets and rely on the dedicated work of a few people. Is there a backup strategy?

Well, not that I know of, so let me advance some radical options that may need to be considered should the conservation status of several critically endangered tree-kangaroos continue to deteriorate.

Augmentation of wild populations

The most urgent priority is to increase the population size or, better still, increase the number of populations of the critically endangered species. At present we don't have any reliable estimates but some taxa (e.g. Scott's Tree-kangaroo and the Golden Mantled Tree-kangaroo) probably have less than 100 individuals in the wild. We need to address this urgently because small populations are very precarious. Chance starts to play more and more of a significant role in their survival. A rare event, such as extreme weather (e.g. drought, fire or cyclone) or an outbreak of disease, can send a small population, and hence an entire species, to extinction.

How do we augment?

Captive breeding colonies

One method of augmenting a species is by captive breeding. Most species of tree-kangaroo have been bred in captivity and we know a lot about the specifics of their reproduction, (most recently from the excellent work of Lisa Dabek, Peter Johnson and Steven Delean). So there are no foreseeable technical difficulties in setting up captive breeding programmes to augment the wild stocks of almost any of the subspecies.

With some of the rarer subspecies not presently held in overseas zoos, breeding stock would have to be obtained from the wild and this is always difficult because of political sensitivities in New Guinea. Both the local landowners and the central government would have to support it. A less politically sensitive source of breeding stock might be the hand-raised animals kept in villages.

The greatest difficulty with such an approach is introducing the captive-bred stock into the wild. This is the major problem with almost all captive breeding programmes and many novel approaches have been adopted and much progress made in recent years. However, the long period of maternal care in most tree-kangaroo species suggests that, to survive in the wild, a tree-kangaroo has much to learn before it can be released. This would make captive breeding and release into the wild a very time-consuming business.

Translocation

The problems of re-introduction to wild are avoided if the young tree-kangaroos never permanently leave the wild; that is, if they are raised by their mothers in the wild. Additional wild populations could be established by translocating small breeding groups of threatened species into areas where they were free from threats to their survival.

Graeme Newell considered translocation as a way of alleviating some of the problems of Lumholtz's Tree-kangaroos on the Atherton Tablelands, but concluded that this particular species wouldn't be a good candidate. Under the circumstances, given the resources available in Australia and the present relatively low level of threat facing this species, I think it would be well worth trying. A great deal could be learnt about translocation methods for tree-kangaroos from some carefully monitored trials with a relatively unthreatened species.

Translocating wild koalas onto offshore islands and allowing them to multiply was successfully used as a method of augmenting the mainland populations in south-eastern Australia last century. Several island populations of tree-kangaroos appear to have already been established in New Guinea. There are wild Matschie's Tree-kangaroos living in the mountains of Umboi Island and on New Britain. There is also a population of Finsch's Tree-kangaroo (*D. inustus finschi*) living on Yapen Island, off the coast of West Papua. It is believed that these tree-kangaroos populations were artificially established as these islands have never been connected to the New Guinea mainland.

If some of New Guinea's tree-kangaroo species continue to decline it would be worthwhile trying to duplicate these historic translocations. Rainforest-clad offshore islands in either Australian or New Guinean waters recommend themselves as release sites. If successful, such island populations would ensure the survival of some species should the mainland populations be eradicated. Even if the original populations do survive, albeit depleted, surplus island animals could be repatriated back into their original range to augment the original populations.

Why conserve tree-kangaroos?

Given the threats facing them, it is difficult to see the conservation status of New Guinea tree-kangaroos improving in the short term. Neither the New Guinean nor the Indonesian Government are sufficiently well-resourced to deal with conservation issues, so any initiatives to conserve tree-kangaroos will have to come from Western nations. There are many competing interests in wildlife conservation, so one has to ask hard questions about priorities. Is it reasonable that we spend money on oddities such as the tree-kangaroo? What is so significant about them?

Their case largely rests on their biological uniqueness. They really are one of the gems of the Marsupialia. In the past seven million years or so, which is but a day on the scale of evolutionary time, this lineage of the kangaroo family appears to have appeared suddenly and then, almost as quickly, diversified widely. Their emergence appears to have been a response to the arrival of a new type of tropical forest in Australia, most elements of which jumped the narrowing oceans separating the northward-drifting Australia from Malesia. Therefore, the most powerful argument for their conservation lies in the insights they can give us into the evolutionary history of both the marsupials and the monsoon forests of northern Australia. Perhaps even for the insights they can give into the processes of evolution itself. Someday, perhaps, some young scientist will be so moved by these quixotic beasts to pose audacious questions, such as: are these the primates of the Marsupialia?

Appendix
Basic information for each species

(based on Flannery et al. 1996 and Betz 2001)

Australia

Dendrolagus bennettianus (Bennett's Tree-kangaroo)

Body weight: males: 11.5–13.7 kg; females: 7.5–10.6 kg

Main habitat: closed forest, various types ranging from lowland, monsoon forest to montane rainforest

Subspecies: none

Distribution: north-east Queensland, north of the Daintree River to Mount Amos area, west from Coral Sea coast to the Windsor Tablelands

Dendrolagus lumholtzi (Lumholtz's Tree-kangaroo)

Body weight: males. 8.6 kg (av.); females: 7.1 kg (av.)

Main habitat: upland closed forest

Subspecies: none

Distribution: north-east Queensland, from Cardwell Range and Atherton Tablelands north to the Mount Carbine Tablelands

New Guinea

Dendrolagus inustus (Grizzled Tree-kangaroo)

Body weight: males: to 17 kg (15.5 kg av.); females: 11.4 kg (av.)

Main habitat: ? low and middle elevation rainforest

Subspecies: 2

Distribution: *D. i. inustus*, West Papua only, mainly on Vogelkopt, Bomberai and Wandammen Peninsulas

D. i. finschi, north coast of New Guinea from approximate location of Wewak westwards to Van Rees Mountains and Yapen Island in West Papua

Dendrolagus ursinus (Vogelkopt or White-throated Tree-kangaroo)
    Body weight: males: ?; females: ?
    Main habitat: closed forest, from middle elevations up to mossy upland forest
    Subspecies: none
    Distribution: endemic to West Papua; occurs on Vogelkopt and Bomberai Peninsulas as well as around the southern coast to Etna Bay

Dendrolagus goodfellowi (Goodfellow's Tree-kangaroo)
    Body weight: males: 8.0–9.5 kg; females: 7.0–8.5 kg
    Main habitat: lower to mid-montane rainforests, especially *Castanopsis* (Oak) -rich forests
    Subspecies: 3
    Distribution: *D. g. goodfellowi*, southern end of the Central Cordillera, primarily in the Owen Stanley and Bowutu Mountains
              D. g. buerguersi, western end of the Central Cordillera, finishing near the West Papuan border
              D. g. pulcherrimus, Bewani and Torricelli Mountains, North Coastal Ranges

Dendrolagus matschiei (Huon or Matschie's Tree-kangaroo)
    Body weight: males: 8.0–10.0 kg; females: 8.4–10.5 kg
    Main habitat: upland rainforest
    Subspecies: none
    Distribution: Finisterre, Saruwaged, Cromwell and Rawlinson Mountains of the Huon Peninsula, north-east Papua New Guinea as well as two nearby offshore islands, Umboi and New Britain (Mount Agulupella)

Dendrolagus spadix (Lowland Tree-kangaroo)
    Body weight: males: 7.0–9.1 kg; females: ?
    Main habitat: lowland rainforest, swamp forest.
    Subspecies: none
    Distribution: lowlands of southern Papua New Guinea, east of Lake Murray to at least the Purari River, Great Papuan Plateau

Dendrolagus dorianus-complex (Doria's, Scott's Tree-kangaroos and dingiso)
    Body weight: males: 9.0–4.5 kg; females: 8.0–10.5 kg
    Main habitat: mossy mid- to upper-montane forests
    Species/ currently 3 species and 7 subspecies recognised
    subspecies:

Distribution: *D. d. dorianus*, south-east Papua New Guinea, Owen Stanley Mountains

D. d. notatus, Central Highlands from Wau to Strickland River, Papua New Guinea

D. d. stellarum, Victor Emmanuel Range westwards to Wissel Lakes, West Papua

D. d. mayri, Wondiwoi Mountains, West Papua

D. scottae (tenkile), Mount Somoro, Torricelli Mountains, North Coast Ranges

D. scottae subsp. indet. (fiwo), Mount Menawa, Bewani Mountains, North Coast Range

D. mbaiso (dingiso), Snow (Sudirman) Mountains, West Papua

References

Aplin, K.A., P.R.Baverstock and S.C. Donnellan (1993) Albumin immunological evidence for the time and mode of origin of the New Guinean terrestrial mammal fauna. *Science in New Guinea* **19**: 131–145.

Aplin, K.A. (1998) Vertebrate zoogeography of the Bird's Head of Irian Jaya, Indonesia. In: *Perspectives on the Bird's Head of Irian Jaya, Indonesia.* (Eds J. Miedama, C. Ode and R.A.C. Dam), pp. 803–890, Rodopi, Amsterdam–Atlanta, GA.

Aplin, K.A., J.M. Pasveer and W.E. Boles (1999) Late Quaternary vertebrates from the Bird's Head Peninsula, Irian Jaya, Indonesia, including descriptions of two previously unknown marsupial species. *Records of the Western Australian Museum Supplement* **57**: 351–387.

Archer, M., S.J. Hand and H. Godthelp (1991) *Riversleigh. The Story of Animals in the Ancient Rainforests of Inland Australia.* Reed Books, Balgowlah, NSW.

Barker, S.C. and R.L. Close (1990) Zoogeography and host associations of the *Heterodoxus octoseriatus* and *H. ampullatus* (Phthiraptera: Boopiidae) from rock-wallabies (Marsupialia: Petrogale). *International Journal for Parasitology* **20**: 1081–1087.

Barlow B.A. and B.P.M. Hyland (1988) The origins of the flora of Australia's wet tropics. *Proceedings of the Ecological Society of Australia* **15**: 1–17.

Barrett, C. (1923) *Rambles Around the Zoo.* Whitcombe & Tombs Ltd, Melbourne.

Baverstock, P.R., B.J. Richardson, J. Birrell and M. Krieg (1989) Albumin immunologic relationships of the Macropodidae (Marsupialia). *Systematic Zoology* **38**: 38–50.

Beddard, F.E. (1895) On the visceral anatomy and brain of *Dendrolagus bennettianus*. *Proceedings of the Zoological Society (London)* **XI**: 131–137.

Betz, W. (2001) Matschie's Tree-kangaroo (Marsupialia: Macropodidae, *Dendrolagus matschiei*) in Papua New Guinea: Estimates of population density and landowner accounts of food plants and natural history. MPhil thesis, University of Southhampton.

Beveridge, I. (1997) *Macropostrongyloides dendrolagi* n. sp., and *Mbaisonema coronatum* n. g., n. sp., two new species of nematodes (Strongyloidea: Cloacinidae) from tree-kangaroos, *Dendrolagus* spp. (Marsupialia: Macropodidae) from Irian Jaya, Indonesia. *Systematic Parasitology* **38**: 25–31.

Beveridge, I. (2002) New species and new records of *Cloacina* von Linstow, 1898 (Nematoda: Strongyloidea) parasitic in macropodid marsupials from Papua New Guinea. *Records of the South Australian Museum* **35**: 1–32

Beveridge, I. and P.M. Johnson (2004) Cestode parasites of tree-kangaroo (*Dendrolagus* spp.: *Marsupialia*) with the description of two new species of *Progamaotaenia* (Cestoda: Anoplocephalidae). *Transactions of the Royal Society of South Australia* **128**: 175–185.

Bishop, N. (1997) Functional anatomy of the Macropodid Pes. *Proceedings of the Linnaen Society of New South Wales* **117**: 17–50.

Bowyer, J.C., G.R. Newell, C.J. Metcalfe and M.B.D. Eldridge (2003) Tree-kangaroos *Dendrolagus* in Australia: are *D. lumholtzi* and *D. bennettianus* sister taxa? *Australian Zoologist* **32**: 207–213.

Brass, L.J. (1953) Results of the Archbold Expedition no. 68. Summary of the Cape York (Australia) Expedition. *Bulletin of the American Museum of Natural History* **102**.

Breeden, S. and K. Breeden (1970) *Tropical Queensland*. Collins, Sydney.

Bulmer, R.N.H. and J.I. Menzies (1972) Karam classification of Marsupials and Rodents. *Journal of the Polynesian Society* **82**: 472–499.

Cairn, E.J. and R. Grant (1890) Report of a collecting trip to north-eastern Queensland during April to September 1889. *Records of the Australian Museum* **1**: 27–31.

Campeau-Peloquin, A., J.W. Kirsch, M.D.B. Eldridge and F-J. Lapointe (2001) Phylogeny of the rock-wallabies, *Petrogale* Marsupialia: Macropodidae) based on DNA/DNA hybridisation. *Australian Journal of Zoology* **49**: 463–486.

Collett, R. (1884) On some apparently new Marsupials from Queensland. *Proceedings of the Zoology Society (London)* **XXVI**: 381–388.

Covacevich, J. (2003) First formal Australian record of a tree-kangaroo: Aboriginal not Australian. *Journal of Aboriginal History* **26**: 220–222.

Crisp, M.D., J.G. West and H.P. Linder (1999) Biogeography of the terrestrial flora. In: *Flora of Australia*, Vol. 1. 2nd edn, pp. 321–367. CSIRO Publishing/ABRS, Melbourne.

Dart, R.A. (1925) *Australopithecus africanus*: the man-ape of South Africa. *Nature* **115**, 195-199.

Dabek L. and M. Hutchins (1990) The social biology of tree-kangaroos: implications for captive management. In: *The Biology and Management of Tree-kangaroos*, (Eds M. Roberts and M. Hutchins), pp. 17–20. AAZPA Marsupial and Monotreme Advisory Group Bulletin 1.

Dabek, L. (1995) The reproduction biology and behaviour of captive female Matschie's tree-kangaroo (*Dendrolagus matschiei*). PhD dissertation, University of Washington, Seattle.

De Vis, C.W. (1887) Notice of a probable new species of *Dendrolagus*. *Proceedings of the Royal Society of Queensland* **3**: 11–14.

De Vis, C.W. (1888) On a third species of the Australian tree-kangaroo. *Proceedings of the Royal Society of Queensland* **4**: 132–134.

Egerton, J.R. (1963) Melioidosis in a tree climbing kangaroo. *Australian Veterinary Journal* **39**: 243–244.

Eldredge, N. and S.J. Gould (1972) Punctuated equilibria: an alternative to phyletic gradualism. In: *Models in Paleobiology*, (Ed T.J.M. Schopf), pp. 82–115, Freeman Cooper and Company, San Francisco.

Eldridge, M.D.B. and R. L. Close (1994) Chromosomes and evolution in Rock-wallabies *Petrogale* (Marsupialia: Macropodidae). *Australian Mammalogy* **19**: 123–135.

Flannery, T.F. (1990) *Mammals of New Guinea*. Robert Brown and Associates, Carina, Brisbane.

Flannery, T.F. (1993) Taxonomy of *Dendrolagus goodfellowi* (Macropodidae: Marsupialia) with description of a new species. *Records of the Australian Museum* **45**: 33–42.

Flannery, T.F. (1996) Conservation. In: *Tree-kangaroos: A Curious Natural History* (T.F. Flannery, R.W. Martin and A. Szalay). pp. 84–88. Reed Books, Melbourne.

Flannery, T.F. and F. Szalay (1982) *Bohra paulae*, a new giant fossil tree kangaroo (Marsupialia:Macropodidae) from New South Wales, Australia. *Australian Mammalogy* **5**: 83–94.

Flannery, T.F., and M. Archer (1984) The Macropodoids (Marsupialia) of the early Pliocene Bow Local Fauna, Central Eastern New South Wales. *Australian Zoologist* **21**: 357–383.

Flannery, T.F. and L. Seri (1990) *Dendrolagus scottae n. sp.* (Marsupialia: Macropodidae) a new tree-kangaroo from Papua New Guinea. *Records of the Australian Museum* **42**: 237–245.

Flannery, T.F., M-J. Mountain and K. Aplin (1983) Quarternary kangaroos (Macropodidae: Marsupialia) from Nombe rock shelter, Papua New Guinea, with comments on the nature of megafaunal extinctions in the New Guinea Highlands. *Proceedings of the Linnean Society of New South Wales* **107**: 75–97.

Flannery, T.F., Boeadi and A. Szalay (1995) A new tree-kangaroo (*Dendrolagus*: Marsupialia) from Irian Jaya, Indonesia, with notes on ethnography and the evolution of tree-kangaroos. *Mammalia* **59**: 65–84.

Flannery, T.F., T.H. Rich, W.D. Turnbull and E.L. Lundelius (1992) The Macropodidae (Marsupialia) of the early Pliocene Hamilton local fauna, Victoria. *Fieldiana, Geology* **25** (n. s).

Flannery, T.F., R.W. Martin and A. Szalay (1996) *Tree-kangaroos: A Curious Natural History*. Reed Books, Melbourne.

Ganslosser, U. (1977) Observations on the behaviour of Doria's Tree-kangaroos and Grizzled Tree-kangaroos in Zoological Gardens. *Zoologischer Anzeiger* **198**: 393–412.

Ganslosser, U. (1980) A study of vertical climbing in some species of Tree-kangaroo (*Dendrolagus*, Marsupialia). *Zoologischer Anzeiger* **205**: 43–66.

Ganslosser, U. (1981) A study of vertical climbing in some species of Tree-kangaroo (*Dendrolagus*, Marsupialia). II. Temporal and spatial sequences during climbing. *Zoologischer Anzeiger* **206**: 62–86.

George, G.G. (1977) Up a tree with kangaroos. *Animal Kingdom* April/May: 20–24.

George, G.G. (1978) The status of endangered Papua New Guinea mammals. In: *The Status of Endangered Australasian Wildlife*, (Ed M.J. Tyler), pp. 93–100, The Royal Zoological Society of South Australia, Adelaide.

George, G.G. (1982) Tree-kangaroos (*Dendrolagus* spp.): their management in captivity. In: *The Management of Australian Mammals in Captivity*, (Ed D.D. Evans), pp. 102–107, The Zoological Board of Victoria, Melbourne.

Gould, S.J. (1983) The episodic nature of evolutionary change. In: *The Panda's Thumb: More Reflections on Natural History*, pp. 149–154, Penguin Books, Harmondsworth, UK.

Groves, C.P. (1982) The sytematics of tree kangaroos (*Dendrolagus*; Marsupialia, Macropodidae). *Australian Mammalogy* **5**: 157–186.

Groves, C.P. (1990) The centrifugal pattern of speciation in Meganesian rainforest mammals. *Memoirs of the Queensland Museum* **28**: 325–328.

Heath A., K. Benner and J. Watson-Jones (1990) Husbandry and management of Matschie's Tree-kangaroo: a case study. In: *The Biology and Management of Tree-kangaroos*, (Eds M. Roberts and M. Hutchins), pp. 25–32, AAZPA Marsupial and Monotreme Advisory Group Bulletin 1.

Horsup, A. and H. Marsh (1992) The diet of the Allied rock wallaby in the Wet-Dry tropics. *Wildlife Research* **19**: 17–33.

Husson, A.M and F.W. Rappard (1958) Note on the mammal and habits of *Dendrolagus ursinus* and *D. leucogenys* Matschie (Mammalia: Marsupialia). *Nova Guinea* N. S. **9**: 9–14.

Husson, A.M. (1955) Notes on mammals collected by the Swedish New Guinea Expedition 1948–49. *Nova Guinea N. S.* **6**: 2283–2306.

Hyland, B.P.M. and T. Whiffin (1993). *Australian Tropical Rainforest Trees: An Interactive Identification System*. Vol. 1, 303 pp.; Vol. 2, 564 pp., CSIRO, Australia.

IUCN (2004) *IUCN Red List of Threatened Species* (www.redlist.org).

Iwanuik, A.N., J.E. Nelson, S.M. Pellis and I.Q. Whishaw (1998) Reaching, grasping and manipulation of food objects by two tree-kangaroo species, *Dendrolagus lumholtzi* and *D. matschiei. Australian Journal of Zoology* **46**: 235–248.

Jacobs, M. (1988) *The Tropical Rainforest: A First Encounter*. Springer-Verlag, Berlin.

Johnson, P.M. and S. Delean (2003) Reproduction of Lumholtz's tree-kangaroo, *Dendrolagus lumholtzi* (Marupialia: Macropodidae) in captivity, with age estimation and development of pouch young. *Wildlife Research* **30**: 505–512.

Johnson, P.M., M. Hawkes and S. Sullivan (2002) Predation by Lumholtz's Tree-kangaroos *Dendrolagus lumholtzi* in captivity. *Thylacinus* **26**: 6–7.

Johnston, T.H. and C.D. Gillies (1918) Notes on records of tree-kangaroos in Queensland. *Australian Zoologist* **1**: 153–156.

Jones, H.I. (1979) Gastrointestinal nematodes, including three new species, from Australian and Papua and New Guinean Pythons. *Proceedings of the Helminthology Society, Washington* **46**: 1–14.

Jones, K.M.W. (2001) Tree-kangaroo (*Dendrolagus* spp.): Faecal analysis as a technique to determine food plants and feeding patterns. Honours thesis, Department of Environmental Biology, University of Adelaide.

Kanowski, J. and N.I.J. Tucker (2002) Trial of shelter poles to aid the dispersal of tree-kangaroos on the Atherton Tablelands, north Queensland. *Ecological Management and Restoration* **3**: 137–138.

Kanowski J., L. Felderhof, G. Newell, T. Parker, C. Schmidt, B. Stirn, R. Wilson and J. Winter (2001) Community survey of the distribution of Lumhotlz's Tree-kangaroo on the Atherton Tablelands, north-east Queensland. *Pacific Conservation Biology* **7**: 79–86.

Kanowski, J., M.S. Hopkins, H. Marsh and J.W. Winter (2001) Ecological correlates of folivore abundance in north Queensland rainforest. *Wildlife Research* **28**: 1–8.

Kirsch J.A., F-J. Lapointe and A. Foeste (1995) Resolution of portions of the kangaroo phylogeny (Marsupialia: Macropodidae) using DNA hybridization. *Biological Journal of the Linnean Society* **55**: 309–328.

Kirsch J.A., F-J. Lapointe and M.S. Springer (1997) DNA-hybridization studies of marsupials and their implications for metatherian classification. *Australian Journal of Zoology* **45**: 211–280.

Le Souef, W.H.D. (1894) A trip to North Queensland. *The Victorian Naturalist* **11**: 3–29.

Le Souef, W.H.D. (1897) Ascent of Mt. Peter Botte, North Queensland. *The Victorian Naturalist* **14**: 151–167.

Le Souef, W.H.D. (1907) *Wildlife in Australia*. Whitcombe and Tombs Ltd, Christchurch.

Le Souef, W.H.D. (1922) *Wild Life in Australia*. Whitcombe and Tombs Ltd, Christchurch.

Lewin, R.A. (1999) *Merde. Excursions Into Scientific, Cultural and Sociohistorical Coprology*. Aurum Press, London.

Lonnberg, E. and E. Mjoberg (1916) Results of Dr E. Mjoberg's Swedish Scientific Expedition to Australia 1910–13. II. Mammals from Queensland. *Kunglinger Svenska Vetenskapsakademiens Handlingar* **52**: 1–11.

Lumholtz, C. (1884) Notes upon some mammals recently discovered in Queensland. *Proceedings of the Zoology Society (London)* 406–409.

Lumholtz, C. (1889) *Among Cannibals.* J. Murray, London (facsimile edition, Australian National University Press, Canberra, 1980).

Martin, R.W. (1992) An ecological study of Bennett's Tree-kangaroo (*Dendrolagus bennettianus*). *Project 116.* World Wide Fund for Nature, Sydney, Australia.

Martin, R.W. (1995) Ecological studies of Bennett's Tree-kangaroo. Abstract: Annual Scientific Meeting of the Australian Mammal Society, Townsville, September 1995. Unpublished.

Martin, R.W. (1995) Field observation of predation on Bennett's Tree-kangaroo (*Dendrolagus bennettianus*) by an Amethystine Python (*Morelia amethistina*). *Herpetological Review* **26**: 74–76.

Martin, R.W. (1996) Tcharibeena: Field studies of Bennett's Tree-kangaroo. In: *Tree-kangaroos: A Curious Natural History* (T.F. Flannery, R. Martin and A. Szalay), pp. 36–65, Reed Books, Melbourne.

Menzies, J.I. (1992) A tree-kangaroo (*Dendrolagus* sp.) from the highlands of western New Guinea. *Science in New Guinea* **18**: 94.

Mjoberg E. (1919) Preliminary description of a new family and three new species of *Mallophaga. Entomologisk Tidskrift* **40**: 93–96.

Nelson, J., H. Stephan and G. Barron (in press) *Comparative Brain Research in Mammals.* Vol. III. *Marsupialia.*

Newell, G.R. (1999) Australia's tree-kangaroos: current issues in their conservation. *Biological Conservation* **87**: 1–12.

Newell, G.R. (1999) Home range and habitat use by Lumholtz's tree-kangaroo (*Dendrolagus lumholtzi*) within a rainforest fragment in north Queensland. *Wildlife Research* **26**: 129–145.

Newell, G.R. (1999) Responses of Lumholtz's tree-kangaroo (*Dendrolagus lumholtzi*) to loss of habitat within a tropical rainforest fragment. *Biological Conservation* **91**: 181–189.

Nightingale, N. (1992) Land of the big pigeon. *BBC Wildlife* **10**: 44–50.

Owen, R. (1852) Notes on the anatomy of the tree-kangaroo (*Dendrolagus inustus* Gould). *Proceedings of the Zoological Society (London)* **1852**: 103–107.

Pahl, L.I., J.W. Winter and G. Heinsohn (1988) Variation in responses of arboreal marsupials to fragmentation of tropical rainforest in north eastern Australia. *Biological Conservation* **46**: 71–82.

Pasveer, J.M. and K.P. Aplin (1998) Late Pleistocene to modern vertebrate faunal succession and environmental change in lowland New Guinea: Evidence from the Bird's Head of Irian Jaya, Indonesia. In: *Perspectives on the Bird's Head of Irian Jaya, Indonesia*, (Eds J. Miedama, C. Ode and R.A.C. Dam), pp. 890–930, Rodopi, Amsterdam–Atlanta, GA

Proctor-Grey, E. (1985) The behavior and ecology of Lumholtz's Tree-kangaroo *Dendrolagus lumholtzi* (Marsupialia: Macropodidae). PhD thesis, Harvard University.

Quammen, D. (1997) *The Song of the Dodo: Island Biogeography in an Age of Extinctions.* Touchstone Books, New York.

Ramsay, E.P. (1883) Contributions to the zoology of New Guinea. *Proceedings of the Linnean Society of New South Wales* **VIII**: 17–29.

Ray, N. and J.M. Adams. (2001) A GIS-based vegetation map of the world at the last glacial maximum (25,000–15,000 BP). *Internet Archaeology* 11<http://intarch. ac.uk/journal/issue11/rayadams_toc. html>

Rothschild W., and N.C. Rothschild (1898) Descriptions of three new kangaroos, and notes on the skull of *Dendrolagus bennettianus. Novitates Zoologicae* **5**: 511–513.

Rothschild W., and G. Dollman (1933) A new tree-kangaroo from the Wondiwoi Mountains, Dutch New Guinea. *Proceedings of the Zoological Society (London)* **1933**: 40.

Rothschild W., and G. Dollman (1936) The Genus *Dendrolagus. Transactions of the Zoological Society (London)* **XXI**: 477–548.

Schlegel, H. and S. Muller (1845) Over drie buideldieren uit de familie der Kengoeroe's. In: *Verhandelingen over de Natuurlijke der Nederlandsche Overzeesche Bezittingen*, (Ed C.J. Temminck), pp. 129–148, Leiden.

Schodde, R. (1989) Origins, radiations and sifting in the Australian biota: changing concepts from new data and old. *Australian Systematic Botany Society Newsletter* **60**: 10–21.

Seebeck, J. and I. Mansergh (1998) Mammals introduced to Wilson's Promontory. *The Victorian Naturalist* **115**: 350–356.

Seebohn, H. (1894) On additions to the menagerie. *Proceedings of the Zoological Society (London)* 693.

Semon, R. (1899) *In the Australian Bush and on the Coast of the Coral Sea: Being the Experiences and Observations of a Naturalist in Australia, New Guinea and the Moluccas.* Macmillan and Co. Ltd, London.

Sprent, J.F.A. (1963) The life history and development of *Amplicaecum robertsi*, an ascaridoid parasite of the carpet snake. *Parasitology* **53**: 321–327.

Sprent, J.F.A. and E.A. McKeown (1979) Studies on ascaridoid nematodes in pythons: development in the definitive host. In: *Dynamic Aspects of Host-Parasite Relationships*, (Ed A. Zuckerman), Vol. III, Israel University Press, Jerusalem.

Strahan, R. (1981) *A Dictionary of Australian Mammal Names.* Angus and Robertson, Sydney.

Tate, G.H. (1948) Results of the Archbold Expedition no. 59. Studies on the anatomy and phylogeny of the Macropodidae (Marsupialia). *Bulletin of the American Museum of Natural History* **91**: 233–357.

Tracey, J.G. (1982) *The Vegetation of the Humid Tropical Region of North Queensland.* CSIRO, Melbourne.

von Keler, S. (1971) A revision of the Australian Boopiidae (Insecta: Phthiraptera) with notes on the Trimenopoinidae). *Australian Journal of Zoology*, Supplementary Series, Supplement 6.

Waite, E.R. (1894) Observations on *Dendrolagus bennettianus* De Vis. *Proceedings of the Linnean Society of New South Wales* **IX**: 571–582.

Wallace, A.R. (1962) *The Malay Archipelago.* Dover Publications Inc, New York (an unabridged republication of the 1869 Macmillan and Company, London edition).

Wegener, A. (1915) *Die Entstehung der Kontinente und Ozeane.* Sammlung Vieweg, Brunswick.

White, M.E. (1994) *After the Greening: The Browning of Australia.* Kangaroo Press, NSW.

Whitten, T. and J. Whitten (1992) *Wild Indonesia: The Wildlife and Scenery of the Indonesian Archipelago.* MIT Press, Cambridge, Massachusetts.

Yeoh, H.H. and Y.C. Wee (1994) Leaf protein contents and nitrogen-to-protein conversion factors for 90 plant species. *Food Chemistry* **49**: 245–250.

Ziegler, A.C. (1977) Evolution of New Guinea's marsupial fauna in response to a forested environment. In: *The Biology of Marsupials* (Eds B. Stonehouse and D. Gilmore), pp. 117–140, Macmillan Press, London.

Index